The **Diabetes-Friendly** Kitchen

The Diabetes-Friendly Kitchen
125 Recipes for Creating Healthy Meals

Jennifer Stack, MS, RD, CDE
The Culinary Institute of America

WILEY

JOHN WILEY & SONS, INC.

Cover image: Ben Fink

Cover and interior design: Vertigo Design, NYC

This book is printed on acid-free paper. ∞

THE CULINARY INSTITUTE OF AMERICA

President	Dr. Tim Ryan '77
Vice-President, Dean of Culinary Education	Mark Erickson '77
Senior Director, Educational Enterprises	Susan Cussen
Director of Publishing	Nathalie Fischer
Editorial Project Manager	Margaret Wheeler '00
Editorial Assistants	Erin Jeanne McDowell '08

Published by John Wiley & Sons, Inc., Hoboken, New Jersey

Published simultaneously in Canada

For general information on our other products and services or for technical support, please contact our Customer Care Department within the United States at (800) 762-2974, outside the United States at (317) 572-3993 or fax (317) 572-4002.

Wiley also publishes its books in a variety of electronic formats. Some content that appears in print may not be available in electronic books. For more information about Wiley products, visit our web site at www.wiley.com.

LIBRARY OF CONGRESS CATALOGING-IN-PUBLICATION DATA

Stack, Jennifer.
    The Diabetes-Friendly Kitchen : 125 recipes for creating healthy meals / Jennifer Stack ; The Culinary Institute of America. — 1
      p. cm.
    Includes index.
      ISBN 978-0-470-58778-2 (cloth)
    1. Diabetes--Diet therapy--Recipes. I. Culinary Institute of America. II. Title.
    RC662.S73 2012
    641.5'6314—dc23
                          2011021095

Printed in China

10 9 8 7 6 5 4 3 2 1

For all food lovers—don't let your passion for food and living be derailed by diabetes. May this book inspire you to take on your health challenges and continue to enjoy good food.

Jennifer Stack

Contents

Foreword

You may benefit from this cookbook if your doctor has told you that your blood sugar level is a little high, you have pre-diabetes, or you have type 2 diabetes. In addition, you will benefit from creating a diabetes-friendly kitchen in your home if your lifestyle, weight, and eating habits put you at risk for developing diabetes. The American Diabetes Association has a Diabetes Risk Test you can take at **www.diabetes.org** to help you assess your risk.

It is possible to feel fine when you have high blood sugar (blood glucose) or type 2 diabetes. Therefore, you might not be motivated to make any changes in your eating habits and lifestyle. However, without any changes there is a high likelihood that your health will get progressively worse. Don't wait for the unnecessary complications of diabetes such as a heart attack, blindness, kidney disease, or amputations to spur you on to develop a diabetes-friendly lifestyle.

Think of your body as a boat. Type 2 diabetes is like a hole in the stern. Ignore it and the water will eventually seep in and interfere with the seaworthiness of your vessel before you reach your destination. You can avoid floating in shark-infested waters if you make repairs and consistently tend to your boat.

There are professionals available with expertise in diabetes prevention and management to guide and support you, but the work is up to you. Your team should begin with an endocrinologist who is a doctor who specializes in the intricacies of diabetes. In addition, certified diabetes educators (C.D.E.) are a multi-disciplinary group of health care professionals such as dietitians, nurses, exercise physiologists, and pharmacists who all specialize in diabetes. Your local hospital may already have a diabetes education program that can put you in touch with these experts.

When diabetes threatens your sense of well-being, learning to cook well and setting up a diabetes-friendly kitchen can be a powerful weapon for reclaiming your health.

Acknowledgments

My passion for food and nutrition started in grade school in Toledo, Ohio. I thought I had created a sandwich combination that would revolutionize school lunches: white bread, margarine, bologna, and an iceberg lettuce leaf. Therefore, I am grateful to my parents, Charles and Marcella Stack, for giving me a college education in dietetics and The Culinary Institute of America for teaching me how to cook. I've come a long way from bologna and white bread.

I am especially thankful for my husband, John J. O'Connor, who keeps my copper pots polished and never complains about cereal and milk for dinner when I can't bear the thought of cooking. He is my best friend and soul mate and his presence in my life keeps me joyful even when life gets challenging.

Bridget Stack, my "go-to" source when I need an inspiration for a party menu, was with me when I made Danish Meat Patties for a project during my dietetic internship. Thank you for laughing with me during that project and through all my life "projects" since then.

My best family meals always occur at the home of Christine and Michael Parker. They nourish their family with more than just nutrients and I treasure my time at their table. I thank them and their children, Sarah, Kelsie, Erin, and Ben for allowing me to test out my theory about "treat-a-ramas."

A champagne toast to Carmela O'Connor who stepped up to the plate during a critical editing phase and gave me the direction and energy to keep going.

Gratitude and dog bones to Hachi-ko, Tiberius, and Miso who have eaten my cooking mistakes over the years. I also wish to marvel at all the barn cats at Cedar Hill Farm who have nibbled a chicken carcass down to nothing and prevented me from making yet another pot of chicken stock.

My appreciation to Mary Davis, for reminding me of the value of low-calorie soups and always being a dear friend and to Susie Eckhardt of Brykill Farm for her friendship, grass-fed beef, and recipe ideas.

Thank you to the team in the CIA Publishing Department, and especially Maggie Wheeler, Erin McDowell, Rob Kristof, Lauren Fury, Eleanor Martin, Jeremy Spesard, and our extraordinary photographer Ben Fink for your positive attitudes and encouragement. It was fun working with all of you. And finally, I'm grateful to my colleagues at the CIA, Chef Richard Coppedge, Chef Bruce Mattel, Chef Hubert Martini, and Professor Steven Kolpan who provided expertise, recipes, and wine pairing ideas.

Introduction

Receiving the news that you have prediabetes or diabetes is a food lover's nightmare. The kind that wakes you up in the middle of the night in cold sweats from watching all your favorite meals being taken away. Diabetes is not a death sentence for fine dining; rather, it is an opportunity to explore cuisines, ingredients, and cooking techniques that are naturally good for blood glucose and health. That is why I decided to write *The Diabetes-Friendly Kitchen* to give you cooking tips and recipes that meet the expectations of the chefs at The Culinary Institute of America, and can improve your blood glucose control and health.

This is not another diabetic cookbook. It is a book with recipes and cooking tips to improve your blood glucose control and reduce your risk for heart disease while still honoring your love for food. It will show you how to make meals that satisfy and meet the standards of the American Diabetes Association and the chefs at The Culinary Institute of America. Making changes in your cooking and eating habits will not happen overnight, and when your motivation and enthusiasm for a diabetes-friendly lifestyle start to wane, good-tasting food can keep you interested and committed. Initially these new meals may not seem as wonderful as any of the fat-, salt-, or starch-loaded foods that you are accustomed to eating. Repeatedly exposing yourself to small amounts of new foods and trying new cooking techniques will help your palate adjust and you may eventually prefer these foods and a healthier lifestyle.

Current recommendations on diabetes prevention and management encourage eating less fat as a way to help you reduce caloric intake and promote a healthy body weight (there is additional emphasis on reducing artery-clogging saturated fats). The clinical research trials that led to a reduction in diabetes risk used the USDA MyPyramid to guide the participant's food choices. Although fat and calorie reductions are appropriate recommendations to help promote weight loss and reduce your diabetes risk, MyPyramid and its updated version, MyPlate, don't necessarily speak the language that intrigues today's foodie. One look at the suggested meal plans from the clinical trials and the food lover is back to watching food television shows for suggestions on what to eat. As a chef and dietitian, I knew there had to be a better way to encourage people to eat healthy. Rule #1: It must taste good. Really good. Not just *OK* or *not too bad.*

Diabetic Scientific Research

The scientific research on preventing and treating diabetes is like a slow simmering broth. It takes time for the flavors of a broth to develop. We monitor, skim, and add the aromatics at just the right time for the desired nuances of taste. Likewise, in research we keep checking in with the studies and look for new insights and understanding. Over the past two decades, the scientific community has followed the results of three major clinical trials: the Diabetes Prevention Program (DPP), the Action to Control Cardiovascular Risk in Diabetes (ACCORD) study, and the Look AHEAD (Action for Health in Diabetes) study.

Here is a taste of the results from these studies.

DPP. Changing your eating and activity patterns to produce a small weight loss (an average of 12 to 15 pounds) can prevent or delay the development of type 2 diabetes in people at high risk for the disease. Participants in the study who consumed fewer calories and fat to help them lose a little bit of weight reduced their risk of getting type 2 diabetes by 58 percent. Part two of the ongoing DPP, known as the Diabetes Prevention Program Outcome Study (DPPOS), is also showing that a little bit of weight loss (5–7% of body weight) and increased physical activity can delay the onset of type 2 diabetes or prevent it altogether.

ACCORD. Changes in lifestyle were more effective than intensive medical treatment to reduce heart attacks and strokes in adults with type 2 diabetes in this study. Lifestyle changes that result in consistently good blood glucose control and avoid spikes in glycosolated hemoglobin levels may be a key to keeping the heart healthy when a person has diabetes.

Look AHEAD. For about eight years people with newly diagnosed type 2 diabetes have been following a program similar to the DPP with part of the intervention designed to achieve and maintain weight loss of 7 percent of their body weight over the long term through decreased caloric intake and exercise. We will be gathering data from this study for many years to come to determine the effectiveness of this type of intervention for keeping the heart healthy in people with diabetes. Some insight gained so far from this study is that flexibility and variety in eating and activity plans is very important. Long-term success with these lifestyle changes is more likely when the treatment is tailored to the individual and revised over time.

What Makes a Meal Diabetes-Friendly?

Diabetes-friendly meals provide a consistent and controlled amount of calories and carbohydrates. They emphasize carbohydrates from whole grains and minimally processed, fiber-rich foods, along with heart healthy fats in amounts that keep the meals satisfying without providing too many calories. Modest portions of lean proteins from fish, chicken, eggs, red meats, tofu, and legumes help make the meals more sustaining.

Generous portions of vegetables are also important to help you stay within your personal calorie and carbohydrate budget. This book includes numerous recipes for flavorful and interesting vegetable side dishes that are naturally low in carbohydrates and calories to help you meet your goals while still enjoying variety in your meals and portion sizes that will satisfy you. The recipes focus on fresh and minimally processed ingredients that are naturally lower in sodium and provide flavor without having to be seasoned with large amounts of salt. Finally, flavor enhancement techniques such as searing, reducing, infusing, and marinating with top quality ingredients coaxes the maximum amount of flavor and enjoyment from the food. When meals taste really good, it is easier to embrace them and a diabetes-friendly lifestyle. We want you to share these meals with others who have a passion for good food and good health. Food, health, life—savor it all.

Creating a Diabetes-Friendly Kitchen

Setting up a diabetes-friendly kitchen and learning to cook well puts you back in control when diabetes threatens your sense of well-being. Preparing your own meals makes it easier to manage your blood glucose and health. A diabetes-friendly kitchen helps you create meals that can prevent pre-diabetes from becoming a full-blown case and improves your blood glucose and health if you have diabetes. Everyone, even family and friends with no health concerns can enjoy the food that comes out of your kitchen, since diabetes-friendly cooking is no different than good cooking of any kind. Good cooking is the art of producing the best flavor in any dish. There are endless opportunities to explore good food and good health, so get started and take the first bite.

Exploring Global Cuisines

Your culinary passion can help you stay committed to balancing the daily "must do" of diabetes management with the "want to do" for your lifetime. Exploring cuisines of different regions of the world can inspire you to try foods and cooking techniques that may not seem appealing in your current eating patterns. You can also keep your meals fresh and new by finding ingredients or cooking techniques that are naturally diabetes-friendly. For example, in many countries vegetables are a regular part of the morning meals where they add fiber while keeping calories low, such as in Israel where a tomato and cucumber salad is often served with breakfast.

Flavor profiles are a snapshot of the specific flavoring ingredients and combinations of ingredients you might find within a cuisine. An Asian flavor profile includes ginger, garlic, soy sauce, cilantro, and lemongrass, for instance; a Mexican flavor profile includes chiles, pumpkin seeds, cilantro, and cumin. (For more about flavor profiles, see the chart on page 71.) In addition, many countries have specific spice mixtures that can help transform ordinary ingredients into world cuisines.

Selected Spice Mixtures of the World

Mixture	Country of Origin	Traditional Use	Form	Characteristic Spices
Bumbu	Indonesia	Used to flavor rendangs and gulais, spicy dishes served with sauce	Dry spice mixture is combined with coconut milk prior to use	Black peppercorns, chiles, cinnamon, cloves, coriander, ginger, turmeric
Ras al Hanout	Morocco	All-purpose flavoring powder	Whole spices ground together	Ten to fifteen ingredients, usually including allspice, caraway seeds, cardamom, chiles, cloves, cumin, ginger, mace, black peppercorns, turmeric
Berbere	Ethiopia	Cure for meats, added to condiments and stews	Ingredients are mixed together, then simmered prior to use	Allspice, black pepper, cardamom, chiles, cloves, coriander, cumin, fenugreek, ginger

Selected Spice Mixtures of the World, continued

Mixture	Country of Origin	Traditional Use	Form	Characteristic Spices
Curry Powder	Southern India	Used to flavor thin, soupy sauces	Freshly ground spices are sautéed in oil at beginning of cooking process	Black peppercorns, chiles, coriander, curry leaves, turmeric, and sometimes cinnamon, cloves, cumin, fennel seed, fenugreek, ginger, nutmeg
Garam Masala	Northern India	Usually added at end of cooking to complete seasoning	Spices are roasted whole, then ground into a powder	Black peppercorns, cardamom, cinnamon, cloves, coriander, cumin seeds, nutmeg, mace
Panch Phoron (Indian five-spice mix)	Eastern India (Bengal)	All-purpose flavoring for vegetable dishes	Sautéed in hot oil prior to cooking	Whole black mustard seeds, cumin seeds, fennel seeds, fenugreek, parsley seeds
Gaeng Wan (green curry paste)	Thailand	All-purpose flavoring, widely used in soups and sauces	Ingredients are ground together in mortar and pestle to form a wet paste	Coriander, cumin, ginger, green chiles, lemongrass, turmeric, white peppercorns
Massaman Paste	Thailand	All-purpose flavoring, widely used in soups and sauces	Ingredients are ground together in mortar and pestle to form a wet paste	Cardamom, chiles, cinnamon, cloves, coriander, cumin, star anise, white peppercorns
Recado	Yucatán Peninsula of Mexico	Rubbed on food prior to cooking; also used as all-purpose flavoring for sauces and stews	Spices are pounded to a paste in combination with vinegar, garlic, and herbs	Achiote, allspice, black peppercorns, chiles, cinnamon, cloves
Five-Spice Powder	China	Used as flavoring in wide variety of Chinese dishes; frequently used in marinades	Whole spices are ground into a raw powder	Anise, cinnamon, cloves, fennel seeds, black peppercorns
Harissa	Tunisia	Traditionally served with couscous	Spices and chiles are ground to a paste	Hot chiles, garlic, coriander, cumin, cayenne, lemon juice, olive oil
Baharat	Turkey	All-purpose flavoring, usually used on lamb, chicken, and fish	Spices are combined and ground into a powder	Black peppercorns, clove, cinnamon, cardamom, nutmeg, cumin, paprika, allspice

Developing Flavor

There are a number of ways that cooks can develop flavor in their dishes. The first approach is to buy foods that are naturally flavorful. Getting to know what's in season in your location, and the purveyors and producers with a reputation for high-quality, hand-crafted foods is an important part of assuring that your meals are as flavorful as possible.

The second tactic is to maximize flavor through proper techniques. Impeccable technique results in foods that have visual, textural, and aromatic appeal. Every technique—from the basic preparation tasks of rinsing, trimming, and cutting, through the selection and execution of culinary techniques like roasting or steaming or stir-frying, and on through the techniques of plating, presentation, and serving—plays a part.

A third tactic is to pay careful attention to how the interplay of flavors, textures, and colors on a plate will affect the flavor of the entire dish. Incorporating fresh, chunky salsa or salads, creamy stewed or braised elements, or adding a crisp item is a key aspect of developing flavor. If there are no contrasting elements on the plate, it is easy to develop flavor fatigue. The first few bites of a dish taste wonderful, but the intensity begins to drop off after a few bites. Many flavoring ingredients don't require any special monitoring to stay within diabetes-friendly guidelines. Toasted, parched, or freshly ground spices and chiles add rich smoky flavors without introducing sodium or fat. Fresh herbs and aromatic ingredients like garlic, lemongrass, ginger, or lime juice add flavor but not calories.

Salting Foods

We used many ingredients and cooking techniques to build flavor in the recipes. We also used salt in modest amounts since the recipes in this book include many whole grains, beans, nuts and seeds, vegetables, fruits, and low-fat dairy that provide important vitamins and minerals that also play a role in maintaining healthy blood pressure.

Adding a little salt can have the effect of bringing out the best flavor in foods. Humans do crave salt because it is essential to the healthy functioning of our bodies, but it has become all too easy to consume far more salt than we need. Too much salt and sodium can have serious and negative effects on our health.

Do not simply eliminate salt, unless there is a specific reason to do so, but use salt wisely. Use regular kosher salt (not coarse kosher), as we have done in our recipes, wherever salt is called for. A half teaspoon of kosher salt has about 560 mg sodium, whereas table salt has 1180 mg sodium since it is a finer crystal and more of it fits into a half teaspoon. (For more information, see Types of Salts, page 5.)

Types of Salts

Salt is found in several forms, each of which carries different qualities. However, all types of salt, with the exception of light salt, are composed of 40 percent sodium and 60 percent chloride.

Table salt is most commonly used in cooking and as a table condiment. It consists of small, dense, granular cubes that adhere poorly to food, dissolve slowly in solution, and are difficult to blend.

Iodized salt is table salt to which iodine has been added as a preventative against goiter, an enlargement of the thyroid gland caused by iodine deficiency.

Kosher salt is granular salt that has been compressed to provide a greater surface area. It is flaky and, compared to table salt, lighter in weight, dissolves more readily, and adheres better to food. Diamond Crystal® kosher salt is formed through an evaporation process similar to that used in the production of sea salt. This is the type of salt used in all our recipes and the nutritional analysis. Coarse kosher salt has a larger crystal and should not be used unless specifically called for in a recipe such as the Caraway-Herb Roasted Pork Tenderloin on page 123. Although kosher salts are typically more expensive than table salt, many chefs prefer to cook almost exclusively with kosher salts.

Sea salt and **bay salt** are collected through the evaporation of natural salt water and consist of thin, flaky layers. They adhere well to food and dissolve quickly. These salts also contain other trace minerals that occur naturally in the waters from which the salts are collected. As such, sea and bay salts from different areas of the world taste different. All are generally more complex in flavor than table and kosher salts. Sea and bay salts can be purchased in fine grain and larger crystal forms.

Stocking Your Pantry and Refrigerator

Using quality ingredients and creating flavor through good cooking techniques will make your meals more delicious. The following pantry guide will help you stock your kitchen with ingredients that are diabetes-friendly. Having these basic ingredients in your pantry and refrigerator makes spur-of-the-moment meal planning easier. We considered the nutritional recommendations of the American Diabetes Association and the Academy of Nutrition and Dietetics when developing this pantry guide and the recipes. But we also kept taste buds in mind since taste is a major motivating factor in what we eat.

You will find fewer refined carbohydrates in a diabetes-friendly pantry and more whole grains and fiber-rich starches. Since people with diabetes are at a higher risk for heart disease, we stressed ingredients that are low in the saturated fats found in fatty cuts of meat, poultry skin, and whole-milk dairy foods, and we avoided all sources of partially hydrogenated (trans) fats.

Another way to satisfy your love of food and cooking is to commit to upgrading some of your ingredients beyond what is typically available at your usual shopping outlets. If you hear of a special seasoning in a cookbook or on your favorite cooking show, seek out a source for it. Even common ingredients like peppercorns and vanilla beans can have wide ranges of quality. Sources for some of the ingredients in this book are listed in the appendix on page 219.

Cooking and Specialty Oils

Canola oil. This neutral-flavored oil is rich in heart-healthy monounsaturated fats. It can be used alone or mixed with a little butter when you want to sauté something and enjoy the flavor of butter without all the saturated fat.

Olive oil, extra-virgin, first-cold-pressed. Taste different brands of olive oils since the place and how the olives were processed will have an impact on the flavor. Olive oil flavor can vary as much as wine so you need to find the brands that appeal to you.

Flavor-infused specialty olive oils. I love olive oil infused with blood oranges or Meyer lemons. When used to make vinaigrette or drizzled over some steamed vegetables, they add a background hint of sweetness. Try olive oils infused with garlic or herbs and spices. If you find ones you love, they can add a dimension to your cooking that can help to replace some salt in a dish.

Nut and seed oils. Walnut, almond, pecan, pistachio, and sesame oil each have their own subtle flavor that is a wonderful addition to any dish that includes these nuts and seeds. For example, a Waldorf salad made with a walnut oil vinaigrette in place of mayonnaise is fabulous. I discovered the flavor benefit of these specialty oils when taking a group of students from The Culinary Institute of America on a tour of La Tourangelle nut farm and oil processing facility in Woodland, California. I store these delicate oils in the refrigerator to help prevent them from turning rancid.

Vinegars and Juices

I try to purchase the best quality I can afford when it comes to vinegar since the flavor is usually less harsh in a quality product. A splash of vinegar in a pot of soup, stew, or in a sauce can brighten the flavor. Feel free to experiment with vinegars infused with fruit or herbs.

Balsamic vinegar. I sometimes drizzle this vinegar onto dishes without blending it with oil, so a high-quality vinegar is especially important here.

Rice wine vinegar. Naturally milder in flavor, it is frequently used in foods with Asian flavor profiles.

Red wine vinegar. I like to use sherry vinegar as a red wine vinegar. The type of red wine grape used will influence the flavor of the vinegar.

Lemon, lime, and orange juice. Keep one or two fresh lemons, limes, or oranges on hand. Bottled lemon and lime juices will not give you the same result. Grating some of the zest off the citrus also intensifies the flavor without adding fat, salt, or calories.

Wine for Cooking

"Cooking wines" sold in the grocery store are poor-quality wines with salt added. These are not diabetes- or flavor-friendly. You do not need to use top quality, award-winning wines in your recipes, just a drinkable wine.

So keeping wine on hand for cooking often means opening a bottle. If the purpose of the wine was solely for cooking, that leaves a big open temptation to drink it because the whole bottle is not typically used in a recipe. Look for some of the more recent higher quality additions to the world of boxed wines, which are packed with a spigot so oxygen never reaches the wine, enabling it to stay fresh for weeks. You can also use just as much as you need for a recipe. Just remember that the boxed wine is in the house to make food taste good, not to make the cook feel good.

Wine has calories and can interact with certain diabetes medications. You need to discuss with your doctor and diabetes team if a glass of wine can be safely included with your meals. Sipping on wine while you cook can lead to too much tasting of the food and eating too much at the meal. You may find it easier to have the glass of wine with your meal only when you are eating in a restaurant since they will closely control your portion and there won't be a good bottle of wine left open at your home.

Vegetables

As much as I love cooking and eating fresh vegetables, life sometimes interferes with my plans and I end up with rotten greens and vegetables well past their prime. To avoid this I tend to keep these hardier veggies on hand. In addition, parsley lasts longer than many fresh herbs, so I wrap a bunch in damp paper towels and keep it in the refrigerator. Add it generously to thinly sliced celery, cabbage, or fennel to make a low-carbohydrate salad.

Broccoli rabe	Carrots	Collard greens	Onions
Brussels sprouts	Cauliflower	Fennel	Spaghetti squash
Cabbage	Celery	Kale	Turnips

Fruits

Fruit can provide some of the carbohydrates for a meal and are a nice addition to salads. Remember to count the fruit as part of your carbohydrate budget. Your blood glucose level may respond differently to a meal with fruit as the carbohydrate as opposed to a whole grain or other starch, so be sure to check your blood glucose level after the meal to determine if the fruit substitution works for you.

Frozen unsweetened berries. These are easy to store and can quickly be added to plain yogurt or oatmeal for a fiber-rich breakfast. It is also easy to create a warm berry dessert with an oatmeal crumble topping.

Canned mandarin oranges and canned pineapple chunks. These should be packed in natural juice and not heavy syrup. Mandarin oranges are very nice added to the Fennel Salad with Blood Orange Vinaigrette on page 151.

Dairy and Eggs

Don't just save the eggs for breakfast and baking. A vegetable frittata or omelet can quickly be made for a low-carbohydrate dinner. The Parsley and Toasted Walnut Frittata on page 33 can be used as an appetizer or a main course.

Omega-3 rich eggs. The hens are fed a different diet, which results in these omega-3 rich eggs. It is not necessary to use this type of egg to keep your diet heart-healthy. (Omega-3 fats are found in fatty fish, walnuts, and ground flaxseeds, too.)

Plain, nonfat, Greek yogurt. This thick, high protein yogurt is great for making a variety of recipes from dips to desserts.

Whole milk, 8-ounce containers. Since whole milk is used in small amounts in some of the recipes, it is easier to have these individual servings on hand rather than purchasing a pint or quart. Aseptically packaged, eight-ounce boxes of can be stored without refrigeration until they are opened.

Canned, evaporated, skimmed milk. This is used in some of the soup recipes in place of cream.

Individual creamers, aseptically packaged. These are useful when you only need a tablespoon or two of real cream.

Unsweetened almond-cashew cream. This rich cream is made from puréeing almonds and cashews with some water. It is rich in heart-healthy monounsaturated fats, and is used in some of the soup and dessert recipes in this book.

Grains and Legumes

Keep small portions of previously cooked grains like pearled barley, quinoa, and brown rice, in addition to some previously cooked beans in your freezer. They defrost quickly and can be added to soups, stews, and salads.

Quinoa. This whole grain is available in different colors. Traditional quinoa is used in the Black Bean and Quinoa–Stuffed Zucchini on page 79 and red quinoa is used in the Chicken, Quinoa, and Parsley Salad on page 109.

Pearled Barley. Although the bran is partially removed before polishing, it still offers whole grain benefits.

Small (7.75-ounce) cans of chickpeas. These small cans provide just enough beans to add to a salad, soup, or side dish. Be sure to rinse the chickpeas first to remove some of the sodium.

Edamame. These soybeans are harvested when immature. They are higher in protein and fat than other beans, and their protein is complete—that is, it supplies all the essential amino acids in the necessary amounts for humans.

Ready-to-eat brown and wild rice mixtures. These are available in ½ cup servings, which can help keep your portions of carbohydrates in control. Be cautious to select only the brands that are low in salt. They should have less than 150 milligrams of sodium per serving.

Whole, multigrain, and high fiber pastas. The flavors and textures vary widely among different brands so experiment until you find one with a flavor that appeals to you.

White pasta. If you keep regular white pasta in your kitchen, consider which shape you can prepare in smaller portions without feeling cheated. For example, one ounce of dry penne or rotelli appears to be a larger portion than one-ounce dry cappellini or spaghetti when cooked.

Whole wheat couscous. Although it is a whole grain, it is more refined than pearled barley, quinoa, or brown rice. Therefore, it may raise your blood glucose more quickly than other whole grains.

Whole wheat pastry flour. This is a very fine flour that produces lighter baked goods than regular whole wheat flour.

White whole wheat flour. This is a new addition to the world of whole grain flours. It is milled from a different variety of wheat so it has a milder taste than other whole wheat flours.

Nuts, Seeds, and Seafood

Walnuts, pecans, almonds, and peanuts. These provide healthy fats and protein but may also be high in salt, so choose the best brand after reading the label. Consider nuts and peanuts as a garnish in your dishes. One tablespoon per portion will add flavor, crunch, and satisfaction to a dish without sending the total fat or calories of the meal over your budget.

Canned tuna and salmon. These convenient sources of protein are rich in omega-3 fats. Experiment with different brands of both water-packed and oil-packed fish to determine the flavor you prefer. Rinsing the canned fish will help remove some of the sodium or you can purchase canned fish with no added salt. Definitely drain the oil-packed fish and consider rinsing it to further reduce the excess fat and salt.

Frozen, plain fish fillets, scallops, and shrimp. These have less sodium than canned fish and are low in fat. They defrost much more quickly than chicken and meats and therefore, do not require a lot of advance planning for a meal.

Advice for Enjoying Beans

Beans are rich in the soluble fiber that helps lower cholesterol levels and slows down the absorption of glucose into your blood. There are numerous types of beans available, each with its own unique flavor and texture.

Beans and digestion. Gradually increasing the amount of beans you eat will allow your digestive track to adjust so gas will not be a problem.

Soaking beans is not essential. However, when I soak beans for a day or two in the refrigerator they cook more evenly and a little faster. Below is a list of some heirloom beans (see photo opposite).

Add salt to the cooking liquid. Don't follow this guideline if you are cooking with a canned broth that is already salted.

Simmer the beans, don't boil beans. This is important to prevent the skins from bursting. If you will be mashing the beans then you don't need to worry about this.

Taste and save the cooking liquid. This broth can be delicious as a soup base even without the beans in it.

Freeze cooked beans. It is just as easy to cook a large amount of beans as a small portion, so think big and cook extra beans that can be frozen for future meals.

Gently rinse canned beans before use. Try different brands of canned beans since quality can vary greatly.

If you really hate beans try the Smashed Calypso Beans with Butter (page 177). The potato flavor of these beans and the butter and chives will convert anyone to a bean lover.

Try heirloom beans. The variety and quality is inspiring and delicious even for non-bean-lovers.

Maxibell. Delicate flavor with refined texture. Try them in salads with fresh herbs and vegetables.

Orca. Mild flavor and hearty texture. Work well in soups and stews with chili, red pepper, and cumin.

Fawn. These beans are members of the rice beans group, so called because of their slim shape. Mix with cooked wild and white rice for a unique side dish.

White Emergo. Also known as sweet white runner beans; they have a creamy texture and are popular in French cuisine.

Scarlet Runner. Big meaty beans that are even better with lots of garlic and wild mushrooms.

Baby Borlotti. These beans are the younger cousins of cranberry beans. They have a sweet, nutty flavor and dense velvety texture.

Calypso. Sometimes called the Yin/Yang bean, they have a distinct potato flavor.

Snowcap. Another potato-flavored bean that is a little larger than the calypso bean but just as versatile.

Organic Maxibell

Baby Borlotti

White Emergo

Orca

Calypso

Fawn

Scarlet Runner

Snowcap

Carbohydrate Curiosity

What type of carbohydrate is best for me? What foods provide this carbohydrate? How much can I have and still keep my blood glucose in a healthy range? When should I eat foods rich in carbohydrate? **The answers to these questions will vary from person to person and even day to day.**

Different types of starches and sweets will affect your blood glucose in different ways. This is referred to as the glycemic response. It is how rapidly and how high your blood glucose rises after eating a specific food. The type and amount of starch or sweets, and what else you eat at the same time, will affect your glycemic response. Stocking your diabetes-friendly kitchen with appropriate sources of carbohydrate requires you to ask yourself some questions.

Testing your own blood glucose level at home with a specially designed meter is one way to help you determine which types of carbohydrate and how much you can tolerate. Self-monitoring of blood glucose (SMBG) may seem like a hassle but it is actually your ticket to freedom from the debilitating complications of unmanaged diabetes. Talk to your doctor or certified diabetes educator about SMBG and appropriate blood glucose levels for before and after your meals.

Use it to help you include some of your favorite foods in ways that will help keep your blood glucose levels normal after the meal. If you are planning to try a new recipe or you want to fiddle around with the amount and type of carbohydrate, testing your blood glucose before the meal and then one to two hours after the meal can give you the feedback you need to modify your next meal, or adjust your medication or physical activity. Your diabetes management team can guide you in making these adjustments to achieve healthy blood glucose levels before and after meals.

Sweeteners

You do not have to use artificial sweeteners just because you have prediabetes or diabetes. When sugar and other sweets are used in controlled portions and part of your carbohydrate budget, they will not raise your blood glucose more than other carbohydrates. However, if you love sweets, you may find it difficult to control your portions of some sweets. Sugar-free foods can sometimes take care of a sweet craving without triggering an overeating episode. You need to honestly assess what sweeteners are best to keep in your pantry to satisfy your cooking and indulging needs without leading to problems with portion control. Remember that sugar-free foods are not calorie-free foods and they often contain carbohydrates if made using flour.

Agave syrup. Agave syrup is a natural sweetener extracted from the agave plant, a cactus-like plant native to Mexico. It is sweeter than white sugar, so less of it can be used for equal sweetness. It is often considered a better sweetener for people with diabetes because it has a lower glycemic impact. That means that you may experience a lower post-meal, blood glucose peak compared to a food with a higher glycemic impact like honey or white sugar. However, consuming too much agave syrup at one time can still raise your blood glucose to an undesirable level.

Artificial sweeteners. Blends of noncaloric, artificial sweeteners, and regular sweeteners are available and may be more palatable if you experience a bitter aftertaste when using only artificial sweeteners. These blends will have some impact on your blood glucose since they contain some regular sugar.

Essential Equipment for a Diabetes-Friendly Kitchen

Even when you are inspired by great recipes and new cuisines, there will always be days when you don't feel like cooking or eating an appropriate meal. You may be stressed, tired, or bored with your meal plan. At these times having a well-stocked pantry and good kitchen equipment makes it easier to rally yourself and make a healthy meal. I rely on certain tools, pots, and pans to help me prepare delicious meals without a lot of advanced planning. Many of the meals could be made without them but they help me get the flavor and results I want without an excessive amount of work.

Cutting Boards

A large (18 by 20-inch) cutting board gives me a large enough work surface to keep organized while having several tasks going at one time. It defines my workspace and keeps me focused.

Smaller (8 by 12-inch) plastic cutting boards. I pull these out and use them on top of my larger board if I am cutting something that might cross-contaminate the rest of the board with germs or intense flavors/odors. I try to save my prep of potentially hazardous foods like raw meats and poultry for the last step when getting my ingredients ready to make a meal. This further reduces the likelihood of cross-contamination.

Knives and Slicing Tools

Your knives need to be very sharp. They should be able to slice through a thin piece of paper without resistance. You are less likely to cut yourself with a very sharp knife because it glides much more easily through the food without you having to force it through. So, along with your knives you need a sharpening steel but you can also consider an electric sharpener or other knife sharpening gadget.

Eight- to ten-inch butcher's knife. A larger butcher's knife is fine if it feels more comfortable in your hand.

Small paring knife. I find it easier to peel round fruits and vegetables with a paring knife instead of a hand peeler.

Serrated edge "utility" knife. The serrated edge makes it easier to cut through breads and delicate vegetables like tomatoes.

Mandoline. I use an inexpensive Japanese brand to create spaghetti-like strands of vegetables and paper-thin slices of vegetables.

Julienne peelers. These peelers are hand tools that create long strands of vegetables similar to spaghetti. This is a great way to make the vegetables at a meal more interesting.

Spoons, Spatulas and Tongs

It is incredibly helpful to have at least two pairs of tongs and two rubber spoonulas. This way I have one to use on raw foods and a clean one for the next task. Having a spare allows me to have two or more things cooking at one time and keeps me from doing dishes partway through the cooking.

Kitchen "locking" tongs.

Large, heat-resistant rubber spoonula.

Heavy-duty, flat, metal spatula.

"Spider" skimming tool. This is a flat, mesh spoon used to skim broths. I also keep a large, fine-mesh strainer for straining large quantities of broth.

Tools for Portion Control

Small kitchen scale.

Measuring spoons and measuring cups. I like to have two sets of the spoons and cups on hand since they are small and not very expensive.

Pots and Pans

Check out the CIA professional cookware for examples of well-made kitchenware.

I do not feel a nonstick sauté pan is essential. Although I want to avoid excessive amounts of fat when cooking, the nonstick pan results in less flavor because the food does not brown as well and develop those delicious bits of meat and vegetables that stick to the bottom of the pan. These browned-on bits are essential to a flavorful pan sauce made with broth or wine. However, I do suggest the following.

Medium saucepan with lid.

Large, heavy, and well-constructed sauté pan. The quality and weight help it to conduct heat evenly and avoid excessive burning. These are usually more expensive but can also be found on sale at various times of the year.

Stockpots. Buy the largest you can store in your kitchen along with a mid-size stockpot

Appetizers

An appetizer, or first course, can signal the start of a special meal. Since portion sizes are usually smaller, you can also enjoy some less-than-ideal ingredients like those high in saturated fats and sodium. For example, the Grilled Lamb Chop with Mint-Parsley Pesto on page 34 is a hearty appetizer that can accompany a vegetarian main course such as the Black Bean and Quinoa-Stuffed Zucchini on page 79.

Appetizers are also a good way to try new foods if you're not sure you want to devote the whole meal to them. If you decide you don't like the Seitan Satay with Tahini Soy Dressing on page 32, your meal is not ruined as you can follow it with a familiar and satisfying main course or soup and salad.

However, appetizers can often push the calorie or carbohydrate content of a meal over your personal limit for good blood glucose control. Sharing one with your dining companions is one way to avoid this. The Silken Tofu and Cucumber Dip on page 23 is great for sharing and an excellent way to start your meal with vegetables by using celery or bell peppers to scoop up the dip.

Another strategy for enjoying these dishes and maintaining good blood glucose control is to use a series of appetizers as the main course. For example, start with the Silken Tofu and Cucumber Dip, followed by the Onion, Walnut, and Blue Cheese Roll-ups on page 29. Consider pairing this with a small glass of red wine (if approved by your doctor).

Roasted Kale and Blue Cheese Crisps

Really large pieces of kale are lightly coated with the dressing and then roasted until dry and delicately crisp. You can also roast kale leaves plain but the blue cheese dressing adds a subtle background flavor that really enhances the vegetable's unique taste. Curly or dinosaur varieties of kale work best for this recipe.

MAKES 6 SERVINGS

6 cups kale leaves, stems removed and packed

½ cup Blue Cheese Dressing (recipe follows)

½ teaspoon sea salt

1. Preheat the oven to 400°F.

2. Tear the kale leaves into large pieces and toss with the blue cheese dressing.

3. Place the leaves on a baking sheet lined with parchment paper and roast until the kale is dry and crispy, about 30 minutes. Toss with the sea salt and serve.

Nutritional Information Per Serving: Calories 57, Protein 3 g, Carbohydrates 4 g, Fiber 0.5 g, Total Fat 4 g, Saturated Fat 1 g, Sodium 323 mg

Blue Cheese Dressing

The silken tofu carries the flavor of the blue cheese through the dressing and the acid from the vinegar helps to lighten the dressing so that it is not too heavy.

MAKES ½ CUP

1 tablespoon walnut oil

2 tablespoons minced shallots

1 garlic clove, minced

⅛ package soft silken tofu (about 3.2 ounces)

¼ cup crumbled blue cheese

1 tablespoon red wine vinegar

1 teaspoon fresh lemon juice, plus more to taste

½ teaspoon freshly ground black pepper, plus more to taste

¼ teaspoon kosher salt

Nonfat milk (optional)

1. Heat the walnut oil in a sauté pan over medium heat. Add the shallots and garlic and cook until soft and slightly browned. Set aside.

2. Purée the tofu, blue cheese, vinegar, lemon juice, pepper, salt, and shallot mixture in a blender or food processor. Thin the dressing with milk, if desired. Season with additional lemon juice and pepper to taste.

Nutritional Information Per Tablespoon: Calories 44, Protein 2 g, Carbohydrate 1 g, Fiber 0 g, Total Fat 3.5 g, Saturated Fat 1 g, Sodium 113 mg

Silken Tofu and Cucumber Dip

If you have never had tofu before, this recipe is a great way to start experiencing the protein-rich goodness of soy foods. Silken tofu performs like yogurt but is not as tart. For the best results, be sure to select silken tofu designed for making smoothies. There is no need to tell anyone this dip is made from something other than yogurt—tofu has a neutral flavor and the cucumber and parsley shine through.

1. Purée the tofu, yogurt, parsley, mint, and green onions in a blender or food processor until smooth. Fold in the cucumbers and tomatoes.

2. Season with the lemon juice, salt, pepper, and 1 tablespoon of the olive oil. Drizzle the dip with the remaining olive oil before serving.

Chef's Note Serve with celery, bell pepper, and carrot sticks.

Nutritional Information Per Tablespoon: Calories 56, Protein 3 g, Carbohydrates 4 g, Fiber 1 g, Total Fat 3.5 g, Saturated Fat 0.5 g, Sodium 125 mg

MAKES 12 SERVINGS

1 pound soft, silken tofu

¼ cup nonfat Greek yogurt

1 bunch parsley leaves (about 2 oz)

1 bunch mint leaves (about 2 oz)

2 green onions, chopped

2 cucumbers, peeled, seeded, and diced (about 2 cups)

2 large tomatoes, seeded and diced

1 lemon, juiced

1¼ teaspoons kosher salt

½ teaspoon freshly ground black pepper

2 tablespoons extra-virgin olive oil

Tahini and Tuna–Stuffed Tomatoes

This tuna salad uses hummus (chickpeas and tahini) to bind the tuna. It can also be used as a spread on a grilled vegetable sandwich, as a dip for raw vegetables, or rolled up on its own inside of leafy greens.

1. Purée the chickpeas, tahini, garlic, green onions, 2 tablespoons of the cilantro, the water, sesame oil, cumin, one can of tuna, lemon juice, chili sauce, salt, and pepper in a blender or food processor until smooth.

2. Add the remaining can of tuna and pulse until the mixture is combined, but some chunks remain.

2. Cut the tops off the tomatoes and take a thin slice off the bottoms so the tomatoes can sit flat on a plate. Hollow out the tomatoes and stuff with the tuna mixture. Garnish with the remaining 1 tablespoon of cilantro.

Nutritional Information Per Serving: Calories 163, Protein 13 g, Carbohydrates 12.5 g, Fiber 3 g, Total Fat 7.5 g, Saturated Fat 1 g, Sodium 182 mg

MAKES 8 SERVINGS

One 15-ounce can chickpeas, drained and rinsed

⅓ cup tahini

1 garlic clove, minced

2 green onions, chopped

3 tablespoons minced cilantro

¼ cup water

½ teaspoon sesame oil

1 teaspoon ground cumin

Two 5-ounce cans tuna packed in water, drained

2 tablespoons fresh lemon juice

½ teaspoon hot chili sauce

¼ teaspoon kosher salt

¼ teaspoon freshly ground black pepper

8 plum tomatoes, or other small tomatoes

Shrimp and Asian Vegetables Wrapped in Rice Paper

These rolls are refreshing and filling at the same time. A version of a classic Asian appetizer, they can be made with a wide variety of vegetables and herbs. The shrimp and vegetables make an excellent salad without the rice paper wraps. Serve this with a drop of pure sesame oil and some freshly chopped cilantro as a garnish.

MAKES 4 SERVINGS

4 teaspoons peanut oil

1 cup thinly sliced shiitake mushrooms

2¼ teaspoons reduced-sodium soy sauce

8 ounces shrimp, peeled, deveined, and chopped

1 cup julienned carrots, blanched

1 cup bean sprouts

1 cup julienned snow peas, blanched

1 cup julienned daikon radish, blanched

¼ cup chopped pickled ginger

⅓ cup thinly sliced green onion

¼ cup Lime-Cilantro Vinaigrette (page 27)

Eight 8-inch rice paper sheets

1. Heat 1 teaspoon of the peanut oil in a large sauté pan over medium heat. Add the shiitake mushrooms and sweat until tender, 2 to 3 minutes. Add the soy sauce and reduce until almost dry. Add the shrimp and sauté just until the shrimp turns opaque. Remove from the heat and chill completely in the refrigerator.

2. Combine the shrimp mixture with the carrots, sprouts, snow peas, radish, ginger, and green onion. Toss with the vinaigrette.

3. Soften the rice paper sheets in warm water for a few minutes. Drain. Divide the shrimp mixture among the rice paper wrappers and roll to encase completely.

4. Heat the remaining 1 tablespoon oil in a large skillet over medium high heat. Sauté the shrimp rolls until golden brown on all sides.

Nutritional Information Per Serving: Calories 261, Protein 16 g, Carbohydrates 27 g, Fiber 2 g, Total Fat 10 g, Saturated Fat 2 g, Sodium 382 mg

Lime-Cilantro Vinaigrette

This vinaigrette is one of the favorites at The Culinary Institute of America and it's easy to see why. The classic combination of lime and cilantro will add a bright, fresh flavor to any dish. It can be used in any salad or even with cooked vegetables so don't limit its use to just this recipe.

1. Whisk the arrowroot with about 2 tablespoons of the broth to form a smooth paste.

2. In a small pot, bring the remaining broth to a boil and stir in the arrowroot paste. Return the mixture to a boil and stir constantly until the broth has thickened.

3. Remove the pot from the heat. Stir in the lime juice and agave syrup and cool completely.

4. Gradually whisk in the sesame and peanut oils. Season with the salt and add the cilantro.

Nutritional Information Per Tablespoon Serving: Calories 32, Protein 0 g, Carbohydrates 0.5 g, Fiber 0 g, Total Fat 3.5 g, Saturated Fat 0.5 g, Sodium 40 mg

MAKES 1 CUP

¾ teaspoon arrowroot *or* cornstarch

½ cup vegetable broth

¼ cup fresh lime juice

½ teaspoon agave syrup

2 tablespoons sesame oil

2 tablespoons peanut oil

½ teaspoon kosher salt

1 tablespoon minced cilantro

Onion, Walnut, and Blue Cheese Roll-ups

These roll-ups are a variation on an onion tart with blue cheese and walnuts. Red wine is a natural with this hearty appetizer. It was paired with Whitecliff Vineyard's Merlot at a vegetarian wine tasting event in New York State's Hudson River Valley. Both the roll-ups and the wine wowed the guests.

1. Preheat the broiler.

2. Peel and quarter the onions and cut into ¼-inch-thick slices. You should have about 6 cups sliced onions. Keep the slices as uniform as possible so the onions cook evenly.

3. Heat the olive oil in a heavy pan over medium heat. Add the onions and sweat, stirring occasionally, until most of the liquid is evaporated, about 15 minutes.

4. When most of the moisture is gone, watch the onions more closely as they start to caramelize and brown. This will happen slowly, so stir the onions as needed so they brown evenly.

5. When the onions start to turn golden, stir in the brown sugar, salt, and pepper and cook until a rich golden brown. Splash in the water, broth, or wine to loosen the browned bits on the bottom of the pan. Remove the onions and keep warm.

6. Divide the onions among the wraps and top with the blue cheese and walnuts. Place the wraps under the broiler for a few minutes until the cheese has melted.

7. Toss the arugula with vinaigrette. Sprinkle the green onions over the walnuts and top with the dressed arugula. Fold in the edges of the wraps and roll up like a burrito.

Nutritional Information Per Serving: Calories 171, Protein 8 g, Carbohydrates 16 g, Fiber 5 g, Total Fat 10 g, Saturated Fat 2.5 g, Sodium 392 mg

MAKES 4 SERVINGS

2 large onions (about 6 cups sliced onions)

1 tablespoon olive oil

2 teaspoons brown sugar

¼ teaspoon kosher salt

¼ teaspoon freshly ground black pepper

1 tablespoon water, broth, *or* white wine

4 small whole grain, high-fiber wraps (about 8-inch in diameter)

3 ounces blue cheese, crumbled

¼ cup walnuts, toasted and chopped

3 cups arugula

2 tablespoons Lemon Vinaigrette (page 30)

2 small green onions, chopped

Lemon Vinaigrette

This simple vinaigrette can be kept on hand to toss with any variety of raw or cooked vegetables or cooked grains, pasta, or legumes. Its flavors pair well with virtually any dish.

Mix together the lemon juice, garlic, mustard, salt, and pepper. Gradually whisk in the olive oil.

Nutritional Information Per Tablespoon: Calories 93, Protein 0 g, Carbohydrates 0.5 g, Fiber 0 g, Total Fat 10.5 g, Saturated Fat 1.5 g, Sodium 170 mg

MAKES ¼ CUP

1 tablespoon fresh lemon juice

1 garlic clove, minced

½ teaspoon Dijon mustard

¼ teaspoon kosher salt

⅛ teaspoon freshly ground black pepper

3 tablespoons olive oil

Quinoa and Nut-Stuffed Portobello Mushroom

The nuttiness of the quinoa complements the earthiness of the mushrooms and is offset nicely by the slight bitterness of the walnuts. You can use a variety of nuts in the stuffing and either red or white quinoa. In addition, you can stuff individual button mushrooms for an appetizer that doesn't need a fork.

1. Preheat the oven to 450°F.

2. Heat the olive oil in a sauté pan over medium high heat. Add the carrot and cook until the carrot begins to soften. Add the shallot and celery and continue to sweat the vegetables.

3. Add the thyme, rosemary, and 1 tablespoon of the sherry vinegar. When the vegetables are soft, stir in the quinoa and add 2 cups of the chicken broth.

4. Bring the mixture to a boil, reduce the heat, and simmer, covered, until the liquid is absorbed, about 15 minutes.

5. Reserve about ¼ cup of the Parmesan for garnish and add the remaining cheese, the nuts, and ¾ cup of the parsley to the quinoa. Add ½ cup of the stuffing to the inside of each mushroom cap.

6. Place the stuffed portobello caps in a small roasting pan coated with cooking spray. Roast until the mushrooms are soft and have released most of their liquid, 10 to 15 minutes. Remove the stuffed mushroom caps and set aside and keep warm.

7. Add the lemon juice, the remaining 2 tablespoons chicken broth, and the remaining 1 teaspoon sherry vinegar to the roasting pan and deglaze. Pour the drippings on top of the stuffed mushrooms. Top each mushroom with the remaining Parmesan and heat in the oven just until the cheese melts. Garnish with a sprinkle of the remaining 2 tablespoons chopped parsley.

Nutritional Information Per Serving: Calories 320, Protein 12 g, Carbohydrates 29 g, Fiber 4.5 g, Total Fat 18.5 g, Saturated Fat 3 g, Sodium 186 mg

MAKES 6 SERVINGS

1 teaspoon olive oil

1 carrot, diced

1 shallot, minced

1 stalk celery, diced

½ teaspoon dried thyme

½ teaspoon dried rosemary

4 teaspoons sherry vinegar

1 cup red quinoa

2 cups plus 2 tablespoons low-sodium chicken broth

2 ounces grated Parmesan

1 cup walnuts, almonds, or pecans, toasted and chopped

¾ cup plus 2 tablespoons chopped parsley

6 portobello mushrooms, stems and gills removed

1 tablespoon fresh lemon juice

Seitan Satay with Tahini Soy Dressing

Seitan has a firm texture and neutral flavor similar to chicken breast. The longer you marinate it, the more it is infused with the ginger, lime, and soy sauce flavors.

1. Heat the olive oil in a small skillet over low heat. Add the shallot and jalapeño and sauté until softened, about 2 minutes. Add the garlic and ginger and sauté until aromatic, about 1 minute more. Transfer the shallot mixture to a blender or food processor.

2. Add the soy sauce, lime juice, sesame oil, honey or agave syrup, and cilantro. Pulse until smooth. If the mixture is too thick (paste-like), add water 1 tablespoon at a time to create a thick marinade.

3. Transfer the mixture to a shallow dish, and coat each piece of seitan. Marinate in the refrigerator for at least 1 hour and up to overnight.

4. Soak 12 wooden skewers in water for 30 minutes. Thread the marinated seitan onto the skewers. Grill the seitan until nicely browned and cooked through, 2 to 3 minutes on each side. Serve with the Tahini Soy Dressing as a dipping sauce.

Nutritional Information Per Serving: Calories 214, Protein 21 g, Carbohydrates 15 g, Fiber 0 g, Total Fat 8.5 g, Saturated Fat 1 g, Sodium 369 mg

MAKES 4 SERVINGS

1 tablespoon olive oil

1 shallot, diced

½ jalapeño, seeded and minced

2 garlic cloves, minced

2 teaspoons minced ginger

3 tablespoons reduced-sodium soy sauce

3 tablespoons fresh lime juice

1 tablespoon sesame oil

1 tablespoon honey *or* agave syrup

2 tablespoons roughly chopped cilantro

12 ounces seitan, cut into ¾- to 1-inch chunks

12 bamboo skewers

Tahini Soy Dressing (recipe follows)

Tahini Soy Dressing

This dressing is great on salads and as a dipping sauce, but it also tastes exceptionally good on a pasta salad as well.

Whisk all the ingredients together until well combined. Chill until ready to use.

Nutritional Information Per Tablespoon: Calories 59, Protein 0.5 g, Carbohydrates 1.5 g, Fiber 0 g, Total Fat 6 g, Saturated Fat 0.5 g, Sodium 123 mg

MAKES ABOUT 1⅔ CUPS

3 tablespoons tamari

¼ cup sherry vinegar

2 teaspoons minced ginger

1 shallot, minced

2 teaspoons brown sugar

2 tablespoons tahini

1 jalapeño, seeded and minced

½ cup canola oil

2 tablespoons sesame oil

2 limes, juiced

Parsley and Toasted Walnut Frittata

The variations on this frittata are endless. Use whatever herbs or finely cut vegetables you have on hand and add some contrast with different nuts or seeds.

MAKES 8 SERVINGS

1. Preheat the oven to 350°F.

2. Heat the walnut or olive oil in a 10-inch ovenproof skillet over medium heat. Add the shallots and sweat until soft.

3. Stir the parsley, salt, pepper, and half of the cheese into the beaten eggs. Add the egg mixture to the shallots.

4. Reduce the heat to medium low and cook, undisturbed, until the bottom of the frittata is firm, about 3 to 5 minutes.

5. Sprinkle the toasted walnuts over the frittata and place the skillet in the oven. Bake until the top of the frittata is no longer runny, 5 to 10 minutes. Add the remaining cheese to the top of the frittata.

6. Allow to cool for 5 minutes. Transfer the frittata to a plate and cut into 8 wedges.

Nutritional Information Per Serving: Calories 137, Protein 9 g, Carbohydrates 2.5 g, Fiber 0.5 g, Total Fat 10.5 g, Saturated Fat 3 g, Sodium 197 mg

2 teaspoons walnut oil *or* olive oil

2 tablespoons minced shallots

¾ cup minced parsley

½ teaspoon kosher salt

½ teaspoon freshly ground black pepper

1½ ounces Manchego or Parmesan, grated

8 large eggs, well beaten

⅛ cup chopped toasted walnuts

Grilled Lamb Chop with Mint-Parsley Pesto

The smoky richness of the grilled lamb and the fresh mint flavor in the pesto makes these chops irresistible. Enjoy one as
an appetizer before a vegetarian main course such as the Black
Bean and Quinoa–Stuffed Zucchini *(page 79)*.

1. Trim the excess fat from the lamb chops. Season with the salt and
pepper.

2. Spread 6 tablespoons of the pesto among the lamb chops.
Marinate in the refrigerator for at least 1 hour.

3. Wipe any excess marinade off the lamb and grill until medium rare,
about 2 minutes per side. Divide the remaining 2 tablespoons pesto
evenly among the lamb chops.

Nutritional Information Per Serving: Calories 246, Protein 14 g, Carbohydrates 0.5 g, Fiber 0 g, Total Fat 21 g, Saturated Fat 6.5 g, Sodium 165 mg

MAKES 4 SERVINGS

4 small bone-in lamb chops

¼ teaspoon kosher salt

½ teaspoon freshly ground black
pepper

½ cup Mint-Parsley Pesto
(recipe follows)

Mint-Parsley Pesto

This recipe is a variation on the traditional pesto and really liv-
ens up the palate.

Purée the mint, parsley, garlic, lemon juice, olive oil, and salt in a
blender or food processor until smooth. Add the walnuts and purée
until well mixed.

Nutritional Information Per Tablespoon: Calories 105, Protein 0.5 g, Carbohydrates 1 g, Fiber 1 g, Total Fat 12 g, Saturated Fat 1.5 g, Sodium 90 mg

MAKES 1 CUP

1 cup mint leaves

1 cup parsley leaves

1 garlic clove

2 tablespoons fresh lemon juice

¾ cup olive oil

1¼ teaspoon kosher salt

¼ cup walnuts, lightly toasted

Soups

Soups are a real workhorse in a diabetes-friendly kitchen. They serve so many purposes beyond a meal in a bowl. Clear broths can be used as a cooking liquid for rice, beans, and grains to maximize flavor without having to rely on salt and fat. Broths can also be splashed into a pan after searing meat or poultry to help deglaze the pan and form a pan sauce. When you simmer lots of vegetables in broth, you create a low-calorie soup that can tame your appetite before a tempting main course. Hearty soups and chowders can be a meal on their own when served with a salad or vegetable sides. Finally, puréed soups are the perfect hiding place for those healthy beans and vegetables that you might not like to eat as a side dish.

Keep various portion sizes (from one cup to one gallon) of beef, chicken, and vegetable broth on hand in the freezer all the time. They are one of the most important ingredients in a healthy kitchen. Some gourmet shops and high-end grocery stores sell frozen house-made broths. When I'm really in a pinch I will use a low-sodium canned broth for half the amount called for and add my homemade broth for the remaining amount; however, canned broths and bouillon cubes have much more sodium (even the reduced-sodium ones) and nowhere near the flavor of homemade broths.

Once you have a flavorful clear broth, you can take the next step and make it heartier with more flavor, texture, and body. Add vegetables that are cut into a uniform size and simmer them in the soup until tender and flavorful. Include leftover grains and meats from a fantastic meal you made earlier in the week or enjoyed in a restaurant. Taste the soup and adjust the final seasoning. Remember that a soup will only be as tasty as each individual component. If you start with a dull, lifeless broth and add flavorless grains and vegetables, the meal will not be as delicious as one that starts with a flavorful broth.

Any time you prepare pearled barley, wild or brown rice, quinoa or another whole grain, or legumes (preferably with homemade broth), make enough to put several half-cup portions in your freezer for future impromptu soup meals. Using a carbohydrate-counting reference, you can approximate the grams of carbohydrate in the individual portion and write it in permanent marker on the freezer bag used to hold the small portions. Depending on how many people you are serving or the amount of carbohydrate you budget for your meal, you can grab one or several of the bags of cooked grains or beans and add them directly to your broth once it is defrosted. This is one of the easiest ways to make a quick and healthy soup or stew that allows you to calculate the amount of carbohydrate in the meal.

The flexibility and variety that soups offer makes them an important part of a diabetes-friendly kitchen. The wide range of flavors and consistencies can help prevent boredom with

Skim away any fat and impurities that rise to the surface of the broth as it simmers.

your meals. They are also so easy to freeze and keep on hand for last minute meals. By limiting the amount of cream, butter, and animal fats, such as chicken fat, in your soup and adding low-calorie vegetables and fiber-rich grains, you can make any soup diabetes-friendly.

Broths

Making delicious broths is an important skill to develop. Whether it's a vegetable, chicken, meat, or fish broth, these flavorful liquids are the secret to great soups, side dishes, and sauces.

You can double or triple the broth recipes and freeze them in small amounts using an ice cube tray or one-cup containers. It's easy to thaw exactly the amount you need. If you freeze the broth in an ice cube tray, you can then transfer the cubes to freezer bags. Each cube is about two tablespoons and is just the right amount for deglazing a pan or steaming vegetables.

The key to the success of many recipes in this book is using good, homemade broths. The investment in preparing the broth will yield many meals that don't rely on excessive salt and fat to make them delicious. For example, the Daikon Spaghetti with Chicken and Tahini Soy Dressing on page 113 and Chicken, Quinoa, and Parsley Salad on page 109 use the chicken that was cooked while making two gallons of broth.

Following is the basic technique for making the broths that we use throughout the recipes. Using this basic technique, you can create your own broth from whatever flavorful ingredients you have on hand. Use a pot large enough to accommodate all the ingredients as the broth cooks and one that is taller than it is wide to allow the soup to cook gently and evenly at a constant simmer. Keep a spider or slotted spoon on hand to skim any impurities that rise to the surface.

Basic Technique for Broth

1. Combine the main ingredients like the chicken or meat in a large pot and add enough cooking liquid to cover the ingredients completely. Bring the liquid to a simmer, skimming the fat and impurities from the surface as necessary. Avoid bringing the broth to a rolling boil, which will overcook the ingredients and cause fat and impurities to be mixed back into the liquid.

2. Add the vegetables, aromatics, and seasonings at appropriate intervals to ensure even cooking time. The herbs, spices, or other seasonings (such as a sachet or bouquet garni) should be added toward the end of cooking time. Continue to simmer until the flavor of the broth is fully developed.

3. Gently remove the meat, chicken, or vegetables from the broth, and then strain the broth through a fine-mesh sieve or cheesecloth. The broth can now be chilled and stored. To help the broth cool down before you refrigerate or freeze it, transfer the broth to several smaller containers and place these containers in an ice bath made in your sink, a very large pot, or even a picnic cooler. Stir the broth frequently to help it cool down to less than 40°F as quickly as possible since bacteria can grow rapidly in a soup that sits at room temperature for more than 2 hours.

Chowders and Bisques

Chowders and bisques are heartier soups whose health benefits can be deceptive. Although they may include seafood and vegetables, they tend to have more saturated fat from butter used to make a roux for thickening, or cream added to the soup for extra flavor and richness. Many times, any thick, rich, and chunky soup, whatever its base, is called a chowder.

Some chowders (such as Manhattan chowder) are actually prepared more like a brothy soup and therefore, do not rely on butter or cream for their flavor or texture. Thickeners, such as rice, white flour, or potatoes, give chowders and bisques their well-known texture. They also add carbohydrates to the soup that may contribute to a rise in your blood glucose. Cooked beans or barley, which have a lower glycemic impact, can be substituted for some of the flour or potato to help thicken a soup and make it a diabetes-friendly chowder. See the Lobster Corn Chowder recipe on page 60; we have modified a standard potato-thickened chowder using beans. Below is the basic technique for making chowders. Use a large, heavy bottomed pot to prevent scorching when making chowders and keep spoons, ladles, and skimmers on hand during cooking time.

Bisques are similar in texture to chowders but they are traditionally based on crustaceans (such as lobster, crabs, or shrimp) and thickened with rice, flour, or bread. Vegetable purées or roux can also be used to thicken the soup. The end result is a soup with a similar consistency to that of a cream soup. When dining in a restaurant, ask if cream has been added to the bisque. It is common to add cream to the bisque before serving, which makes the soup very high in saturated fat and calories. Bisques require the same equipment and similar technique used for making purée soups; however, if using crustacean shells, cook them in fat until they are bright pink or red and remove them from the pan before adding the aromatic vegetables. A finished bisque may also be strained through a fine-mesh strainer or cheesecloth.

Basic Technique for Chowders and Bisques

1. Cook the aromatics until tender. If you are making a shellfish-based chowder, steam the main ingredient until just cooked. Remove the meat from the shells, chop, and reserve.

2. Add the roux at the desired time (refer to specific recipes for more information), and cook just until it takes on a pale golden color. An oil can be used in place of the butter or solid fat when making the roux. You can also try a margarine with no trans fats in place of the butter, but let flavor be your guide because the type of fat is an important component in the overall flavor of the chowder.

3. Whisk in the warm liquid, and bring the soup to a simmer. Stir the soup frequently to prevent scorching.

4. Add the remaining ingredients to the soup at the appropriate intervals to ensure even doneness. Add any herbs, spices, or other seasonings (such as a sachet or bouquet garni) during the final 30 minutes of cooking time.

5. Simmer until all of the ingredients are tender and the soup has good flavor and is thickened properly. If you are using beans or barley to help thicken the soup, add them now and allow them to simmer until the desired consistency is achieved. A portion of the cooked beans or barley can also be puréed to further thicken the chowder. Adjust the final consistency and seasoning prior to serving.

Purées

Purée soups are thick and often have a rustic texture. They are most commonly legume- or vegetable-based, and can be entirely puréed or finished with garnishes for visual and textural interest. The Chilled Beet and Fennel Soup (page 63) is a puréed soup that can be a refreshing change from gazpacho. The Chilled Butternut Squash Soup (page 64) is a flexible recipe that can be served chilled or hot and when fully puréed and strained through a fine-mesh strainer or cheesecloth, can be used as a sauce or in place of gravy. You can add a flavorful broth or other liquid like wine to bring the sauce to your desired consistency. When making a purée soup, it is best to use pots with heavy bottoms to avoid scorching, and have spoons and ladles on hand during the cooking process. While a number of tools can be used to purée the soup (blenders or food processors), an immersion blender allows the cook to purée the soup directly in the pot, saving time and preventing burns.

Basic Technique for Purée Soups

1. Heat any cooking fat in the pot over medium heat. Add the aromatic vegetables and cook over low to medium heat, stirring from time to time, until a rich aroma develops or until they take on a rich, golden hue.

2. Add the liquid (stock, broth, water, etc.) and then add the remaining ingredients at the appropriate intervals to ensure even cooking time. Add any herbs, spices, or other seasonings (such as a sachet or bouquet garni) during the final 30 minutes of cooking time. Stir the soup frequently as it cooks to prevent starchy ingredients from sticking to the bottom of the pan, and skim the soup as it cooks to remove any impurities or scum.

3. Purée the soup and adjust the seasoning and final consistency. The soup should have a thick, coarse texture, but should still be liquid enough to pour easily from a ladle into a bowl. The soup is now ready to be finished or it can be cooled and refrigerated or frozen until ready to serve.

Beef Broth

Beef broth is suitable for heartier recipes. It provides a meaty flavor to a dish without the saturated fat and cholesterol.

1. Season the meat with some of the salt. Heat the canola oil in a large soup pot until very hot. Brown the beef on all sides. Remove the meat and set aside. Add the onions, leek, carrot, and celery and allow to brown, about 7 minutes. Stir in the tomato paste, and cook for 2 to 3 minutes.

2. Return the meat to the pot. Cover the meat and vegetables with cold water. Add extra water, if needed, to cover the meat by 2 inches. Bring to a low boil over medium heat, skimming any scum that rises to the surface as needed.

3. Reduce the heat to cook at a slow simmer. Cover partially and simmer for 3 hours, skimming the foam from the surface as needed.

4. Tie the bay leaf, parsley, thyme, garlic, and peppercorns in cheesecloth to make a sachet. Add the sachet and the remaining salt. Continue to simmer, skimming as necessary, until the broth is flavorful, about 1 hour more.

5. Remove the meaty parts of the beef and save for another use, if desired. Strain the broth and discard the solids. Skim the fat from the surface. Label and date the containers of broth and store in the refrigerator for up to 5 days, or in the freezer for up to 3 months. You can also freeze the broth in an ice cube tray, and then store the frozen cubes in large freezer bags so you can thaw exactly the amount needed at any given time.

Nutritional Information Per Cup: Calories 25, Protein 0.5 g, Carbohydrates 3 g, Fiber 0 g, Total Fat 1 g, Saturated Fat 0 g, Sodium 150 mg

MAKES 2 QUARTS

4 pounds beef chuck, shank, or neck with bones

1 teaspoon kosher salt

2 teaspoons canola oil

1½ yellow onions, coarsely chopped (about 2 cups)

1 leek, white and light green parts, coarsely chopped

1 carrot, coarsely chopped (about ⅓ cup)

1 celery stalk, coarsely chopped (about ½ cup)

½ cup tomato paste

3 quarts cold water

1 bay leaf

2 to 3 parsley sprigs

1 thyme sprig

1 garlic clove

2 to 3 black peppercorns

Chicken Broth

In addition to making chicken broth with the whole chicken, which provides you with cooked chicken meat for other recipes, you can cut a whole chicken into pieces, as shown in the photos, and use only the carcass with the wings attached to make the broth. I like to reserve the boneless breast meat for a different recipe, such as the Chicken Breast Fillet with Moroccan Tomato Sauce *(page 102),* but I cook the thigh and drumstick with the carcass to make the broth more flavorful

1. Place the chicken in a large soup pot and cover with the water. Add water, if needed, to cover the chicken by at least 2 inches. Bring to a boil over medium heat, skimming any scum that rises to the surface.

2. Reduce the heat to cook at a slow simmer. Cover partially and simmer for 2 hours, skimming scum and fat from the surface as needed.

3. Tie the bay leaf, parsley, thyme, garlic, and peppercorns in cheesecloth to make a sachet. Add the onion, celery, turnip or parsnip, salt, and sachet to the broth. Continue to simmer, skimming as necessary, until the broth is flavorful, about 1 hour more.

4. Remove the chicken (which will be falling apart at this point) from the broth. Discard the skin and bones and reserve the meaty parts of the chicken for another use. Strain the broth and discard the solids. Skim the fat from the surface. Label and date the containers of broth and store in the refrigerator for up to 5 days, or in the freezer for up to 3 months. You can also freeze the broth in an ice cube tray, and then store the frozen cubes in large freezer bags so you can thaw exactly the amount needed at any given time.

Nutritional Information Per Cup: Calories 15, Protein 2 g, Carbohydrates 1 g, Fiber 0 g, Total Fat 1 g, Saturated Fat 0 g, Sodium 170 mg

MAKES ABOUT 2 QUARTS

1 whole chicken

3 quarts cold water

1 bay leaf

2 to 3 parsley sprigs

1 thyme sprig

1 garlic clove

2 to 3 black peppercorns

1 yellow onion, coarsely chopped (about 2 cups)

1 celery stalk, coarsely chopped (about ½ cup)

1 turnip or parsnip, coarsely chopped (about ½ cup)

1 teaspoon kosher salt

Remove the legs by cutting between the leg and the breast.

Cut down the backbone to remove the breast meat.

Cut through the knee joint to remove the drumstick from the thigh.

Gently peel the skin away from the meat.

Fish or Shellfish Broth

Use only the bones from mild, lean, white fish, such as halibut or sole, to make this broth. Bones from oily fish, like salmon, will make a broth that is overpowering. The bones must be perfectly fresh. If you won't be able to prepare it right away, store the fish bones in the freezer. Shells from shrimp, crab, and lobsters can be substituted for the fish bones to prepare a crustacean broth.

1. Heat the canola oil in a large soup pot over medium high heat. Add the onion, celery, and leek and sweat until the vegetables are tender and translucent, 4 to 5 minutes.

2. Add the bones or shells and wine and cover the pot. Cook until any flesh on the bones is opaque or the shells turn bright red, 5 to 6 minutes.

3. Tie the bay leaf, parsley, thyme, garlic, and peppercorns in cheese-cloth to make a sachet. Add the water, salt, and sachet to the shells and simmer, skimming scum as necessary, until the broth is flavorful, 30 to 45 minutes.

4. Strain the broth through a fine-mesh sieve or cheesecloth-lined colander. Discard the solids.

5. Allow to cool completely in an ice bath. Label and date the containers of broth and store in the refrigerator for up to 5 days, or in the freezer for up to 3 months. You can also freeze the broth in an ice cube tray, and then store the frozen cubes in large freezer bags so you can thaw exactly the amount needed at any given time.

Nutritional Information Per Cup: Calories 34, Protein 0 g, Carbohydrates 1 g, Fiber 0 g, Total Fat 1 g, Saturated Fat 0 g, Sodium 140 mg

MAKES 2 QUARTS

2 teaspoons canola oil

1 yellow onion, coarsely chopped (about 1¼ cups)

1 celery stalk, coarsely chopped (about ½ cup)

1 leek, white and light green parts, coarsely chopped

3 to 4 pounds fish bones or shells

1 cup dry white wine

1 bay leaf

2 to 3 parsley sprigs

1 thyme sprig

1 garlic clove

2 to 3 black peppercorns

3 quarts water

1 teaspoon kosher salt

Vegetable Broth

Vegetable broth is so quick and easy to make, and the flavor is far superior to that of commercially prepared vegetable broths. Besides making soups, vegetable broth is a flavorful liquid for cooking grains and beans and pan-steaming vegetables.

1. Tie the bay leaf, thyme, parsley, peppercorns, and garlic in cheesecloth to make a sachet.

2. In a large soup pot, sweat the onion, celery, and green onions, and a splash of water until the vegetables begin to release their juices, 6 to 8 minutes.

3. Add the carrot, turnip, fennel, mixed vegetables, the water, sachet, and salt and bring to a simmer, skimming any scum as necessary. Cover the pot and continue to simmer until the broth is flavorful, 30 to 45 minutes.

4. Strain the broth, pressing down on the vegetables to extract the juices. Discard the solids.

5. Allow to cool completely in an ice bath. Label and date the containers of broth and store in the refrigerator for up to 5 days, or in the freezer for up to 3 months. You can also freeze the broth in an ice cube tray, and then store the frozen cubes in large freezer bags so you can thaw exactly the amount needed at any given time.

Note Because the vegetables are strained out of the broth, it has a negligible amount of protein and fat and a very small amount of carbohydrate. It does contain some sodium that leaches from the vegetables into the liquid but this amount is very small because the vegetables are naturally low in sodium.

Nutritional Information Per Cup: Calories 8, Protein 0 g, Carbohydrates 1.5 g, Fiber 0 g, Total Fat 0 g, Saturated Fat 0 g, Sodium 140 mg

MAKES ABOUT 2 QUARTS

1 bay leaf

1 thyme sprig

1 parsley sprig

4 to 5 black peppercorns

2 garlic cloves

1 onion, coarsely chopped (about 1¼ cups)

1 celery stalk, coarsely chopped (about ½ cup)

4 green onions, chopped

1 carrot, coarsely chopped (about ⅓ cup)

1 turnip, coarsely chopped (about ½ cup)

1 cup thinly sliced fennel

1 cup chopped, mixed vegetables such as broccoli stems, zucchini, tomato, mushrooms

3 quarts water

1 teaspoon kosher salt

Wild Mushroom Broth

This broth is so savory and full of umami, it will boost the flavor of almost any dish that it is used in.

MAKES 5 CUPS

1. Add all the ingredients to a stock pot. Bring to a boil.

2. Reduce the heat to cook at a slow simmer. Simmer for 30 minutes, skimming scum from the surface as needed. Strain the broth and discard the solids. Allow to cool completely in an ice bath. Label and date the containers of broth and store in the refrigerator for up to 5 days, or in the freezer for up to 3 months. You can also freeze the broth in an ice cube tray, and then store the frozen cubes in large freezer bags so you can thaw exactly the amount needed at any given time.

Nutritional Information Per Cup: Calories 11, Protein 0.5 g, Carbohydrates 1.5 g, Fiber 0 g, Total Fat 0 g, Saturated Fat 0 g, Sodium 171 mg

8 ounces white mushrooms, finely diced

¼ ounce dried porcini mushrooms

¼ ounce dried shiitake mushrooms

1 green onion

1 parsley sprig

6 cups water

Asian Vegetable Soup

Chef Bruce Mattel of The Culinary Institute of America came up with the idea of the three flavor profiles used for the following three basic vegetable soups. In this one, the edamame and hard-cooked eggs adds protein and the daikon radish "noodles" add substance while keeping the carbohydrate content low.

1. Bring 1 cup of the chicken broth to a boil. Remove from the heat. Add the mushrooms and set aside to steep.

2. Heat the peanut or canola oil in a heavy soup pot. Add the ginger and garlic and sweat until they start to soften. Add the carrot and soften slightly. Add the celery and the white parts of the bok choy. (Use 1 tablespoon of the mushroom soaking liquid, if needed, to prevent vegetables from sticking.)

3. Once the celery and bok choy have softened slightly add the mushrooms and their soaking liquid and the remaining chicken broth. Bring to a boil. Reduce the heat to a simmer. Add the bok choy greens, the cabbage, radish noodles, and edamame. Simmer until the cabbage is soft, about 10 minutes.

4. Stir in the sesame oil, soy sauce, lime juice, green onion, and cilantro just before serving. Serve the soup garnished with the eggs and the hot sauce on the side, if using.

Nutritional Information Per Serving: Calories 85, Protein 6 g, Carbohydrates 6 g, Fiber 2 g, Total Fat 4.5 g, Saturated Fat 1 g, Sodium 441 mg

MAKES 6 SERVINGS

6 cups low-sodium chicken broth

½ cup dried shiitake mushrooms

1 teaspoon peanut *or* canola oil

1-inch-piece ginger, peeled and minced

2 garlic cloves, minced

1 carrot, thinly sliced

1 celery stalk, thinly sliced

½ bunch bok choy, thinly sliced (white and green parts separated)

¼ head savoy cabbage, thinly sliced

½ large daikon radish, thinly julienned lengthwise into "noodles"

1 cup shelled edamame

2 teaspoons sesame oil

2 teaspoons reduced-sodium soy sauce

½ lime, juiced

1 green onion, sliced

¼ bunch cilantro, chopped

2 hard-cooked eggs, chopped

Few dashes hot sauce *(optional)*

Mediterranean Vegetable Soup

This recipe was developed from ingredients I had in my pantry during the middle of the winter. Make this during the middle of summer with homegrown tomatoes, fresh herbs, and fresh basil pesto and the flavors of summer will explode in your mouth.

1. Heat the olive oil in a large soup pot over medium high heat. Add the onion and sweat until it starts to soften. Add the garlic and continue to sweat until the mixture is softened.

2. Add the tomatoes, Italian seasoning, salt, and pepper. Cook until the volume of the liquid released from the tomatoes is reduced by half.

3. Add the chicken stock and bring to a boil. Add the vegetables and simmer until softened. Just before serving, stir in the basil pesto and balsamic vinegar.

Nutritional Information Per Serving: Calories 66, Protein 3 g, Carbohydrates 7 g, Fiber 1.5 g, Total Fat 3 g, Saturated Fat 0.5 g, Sodium 220 mg

MAKES 6 SERVINGS

2 teaspoons olive oil

½ large yellow onion, chopped

3 garlic cloves, minced

4 plum tomatoes, seeds removed and chopped (or one 14.5-ounce can low-sodium, diced canned tomatoes)

½ teaspoon dried Italian seasoning

½ teaspoon kosher salt

½ teaspoon freshly ground black pepper

6 cups low-sodium chicken stock

2 to 3 cups low-carbohydrate vegetables, as desired, cut into similarly sized pieces (see page 130)

1 tablespoon imported basil pesto sauce

1 teaspoon balsamic vinegar

Mexican Vegetable Soup

This soup combines the classic flavors of peppers, tomatoes, and jalapeños into a soup that is both nutritious and beautiful. Cooked black beans can be added to this soup after the vegetables are soft. This will add extra fiber and carbohydrates.

1. Heat the peanut oil in a large soup pot over medium high heat. Add the green pepper and onion and sweat until soft. Add the jalapeño and poblano chiles, garlic, tomatoes, cumin, salt, black pepper, oregano, and dried cilantro.

2. Continue to sweat until the garlic and chiles are soft. Add the chicken stock and bring to a boil.

3. Add the vegetables and simmer until they are soft. Just before serving stir in the fresh cilantro, green onion, and lime juice.

Nutritional Information Per Serving: Calories 63, Protein 2.5 g, Carbohydrates 11 g, Fiber 2.5 g, Total Fat 2 g, Saturated Fat 0 g, Sodium 427 mg

MAKES 6 SERVINGS

2 teaspoons peanut oil

1 green bell pepper, chopped (about 1¼ cups)

1 yellow onion, chopped (about 1¼ cups)

1 jalapeño, chopped (about 2 tablespoons)

½ poblano chile, chopped (about 2 tablespoons)

3 garlic cloves, minced

4 plum tomatoes, seeded and chopped

2 teaspoons cumin seed, toasted and ground

½ teaspoon kosher salt

¼ teaspoon freshly ground black pepper

½ teaspoon oregano (preferably Mexican)

½ teaspoon crushed dried cilantro leaves

4 cups low-sodium chicken *or* vegetable stock

2 to 3 cups low-carbohydrate vegetables, as desired (see page 130)

3 tablespoons chopped fresh cilantro

1 green onion, chopped

Squeeze of fresh lime juice

Chicken Tortilla Soup

This is a heartier soup than the Mexican Vegetable Soup *(page 51)*. The addition of the chicken, cheese, and tortillas make this a meal in a bowl. Consider serving it with the Jícama and Red Pepper Salad *(page 158)*.

(page 51) ... *(page 158)*.

1. Preheat the oven to 350°F.

2. In a small pot, sweat the garlic and onion in a small amount of the chicken broth until the onion is translucent, 4 to 5 minutes. Purée the mixture in a blender or food processor. Set aside.

3. Toast the tortilla strips in the oven until crisp. Set aside ½ cup of the strips for garnish and crumble the remaining strips.

4. Combine the cilantro, tomato purée, onion purée, and crushed tortillas in large soup pot. Bring to a simmer over medium heat.

5. Add the remaining broth, the cumin, chili powder, salt, and bay leaves. Simmer until the soup is flavorful, about 15 minutes. Remove and discard the bay leaves.

6. Purée the soup in a blender or food processor. Serve the soup garnished with the chicken, cheese, avocado, diced tomato, and the reserved tortilla strips.

Nutritional Information Per Serving: Calories 236, Protein 14.5 g, Carbohydrates 25 g, Fiber 4 g, Total Fat 8 g, Saturated Fat 3.5 g, Sodium 355 mg

MAKES 6 SERVINGS

4 teaspoons minced garlic

1⅔ cups diced onion

8 cups low-sodium chicken broth

Seven 6-inch corn tortillas, thinly sliced

¼ cup chopped cilantro

1½ cups tomato purée

1 tablespoon ground cumin

2 teaspoons chili powder

½ teaspoon kosher salt

2 bay leaves

6 ounces cooked chicken breast, shredded

3 ounces extra-sharp Cheddar, shredded

¼ cup diced avocado

¼ cup diced tomato

Chicken Tortilla Soup, served with Jícama
and Red Pepper Salad (page 158)

Chickpea and Chorizo Soup

The chorizo sausage in this soup complements the peppers and adds a spicy, hearty element. The creamy chickpeas add another flavor and texture dimension that make this soup a favorite.

1. In a large soup pot, cook the chorizo until the fat renders and it is browned, about 10 minutes. Transfer the sausage to paper towels and blot off extra fat. Set aside.

2. Heat the olive oil in the same pot over medium heat. Add the onion, garlic, celery, and cumin and sweat until the onion is translucent, 4 to 5 minutes. Stir in the tomato paste and cook, for 1 minute.

3. Add the chicken broth, tomato, chickpeas, corn, red and green peppers, bay leaf, oregano, parsley, salt, and black pepper. Bring to a boil. Reduce the heat and simmer for 20 minutes.

4. Remove and discard the bay leaf. Serve the soup garnished with the cilantro and serve.

Nutritional Information Per Serving: Calories 231, Protein 11 g, Carbohydrates 20 g, Fiber 3.5 g, Total Fat 11.5 g, Saturated Fat 3.5 g, Sodium 557 mg

MAKES 6 SERVINGS

5 ounces Spanish-style chorizo sausage, sliced

2 teaspoons olive oil

½ cup diced onion

2 teaspoons minced garlic

¼ cup diced celery

1 tablespoon ground cumin

2½ tablespoons tomato paste

5 cups low-sodium chicken broth

1¾ cups peeled, seeded, and chopped tomato

1 cup cooked chickpeas, or canned chickpeas, drained and rinsed

1 cup corn kernels, fresh or frozen

¾ cup diced red bell peppers

¾ cup diced green bell peppers

1 bay leaf

½ teaspoon chopped oregano

2 tablespoons chopped parsley

½ teaspoon salt

¼ teaspoon freshly ground black pepper

2 tablespoons chopped cilantro

Shrimp, Bean, and Barley Soup

Two different types of beans add textures and flavors that go beautifully with pearled barley. These ingredients come together with bacon, leeks, and herbs to form a hearty backdrop for the shrimp to shine through.

1. Soak the beans for 8 to 12 hours in enough cold water to cover by 3 inches or refer to page 136 for the short soak method.

2. Drain the beans. Simmer the beans in fresh water until almost tender, 1 to 1½ hours. Drain and reserve.

3. In a large pot, steam the shrimp in the wine. Remove the shrimp, strain the liquid, and add to the fish broth. Remove the shrimp from their shells and roughly chop the meat. Set aside.

4. Heat a large soup pot over medium heat. Add the bacon and cook until the fat begins to render and the bacon begins to crisp.

5. Add the onion, leek, celery, and garlic. Sweat until the onions are translucent. Add the tomato paste and sauté until brown.

6. Add the bay leaf, tomato, rosemary, salt, thyme, pepper, lemon, the beans, and the fish broth mixture. Simmer until the beans are tender, 20 to 25 minutes.

7. Add the barley and reserved shrimp and simmer until the barley and shrimp are heated through, 2 to 3 minutes.

Nutritional Information Per Serving: Calories 340, Protein 24 g, Carbohydrates 45 g, Fiber 11 g, Total Fat 5 g, Saturated Fat 1 g, Sodium 452 mg

MAKES 6 SERVINGS

⅔ cup dried red kidney beans

⅔ cup dried white beans

12 ounces shrimp, shell on

5 tablespoons white wine

6 cups fish broth

1 ounce bacon, diced

¾ cup sliced onion

1¾ cups thinly sliced leek, white and light green parts

¼ cup sliced celery

3 garlic cloves, minced

2 tablespoons tomato paste

1 bay leaf

1½ cups peeled, seeded, and diced tomato

2 teaspoons chopped rosemary

1 teaspoon salt

1 teaspoon chopped thyme

¼ teaspoon freshly ground black pepper

1 lemon slice

1 cup cooked pearled barley

Summer-Style Lentil Soup

The brothiness of this lentil soup gives it a lighter texture so you can enjoy it in warmer months. It is quick and easy to make so don't relegate lentils to just the fall and winter.

1. In a medium soup pot, cook the bacon until the fat renders and bacon is crisp. Add the onion and the minced garlic and sweat until the onion is translucent, 4 to 5 minutes.

2. Add the leek, carrot, celeriac or salsify, and celery. Cover the pot and sweat until the vegetables are tender, 4 to 6 minutes more. Add the tomato paste and sauté until it begins to brown, about 2 minutes.

3. Tie the bay leaf, parsley, thyme, the whole garlic clove, and peppercorns in a piece of cheesecloth to make a sachet. Add the broth, lentils, lemon peel, and sachet to the soup pot. Simmer until the lentils are tender, about 20 minutes.

4. Remove the sachet and lemon strips. Add the wine, vinegar, salt, and pepper. Serve the soup garnished with chives and parsley.

Nutritional Information Per Serving: Calories 237, Protein 14.5 g, Carbohydrates 38 g, Fiber 9 g, Total Fat 3 g, Saturated Fat 0.5 g, Sodium 388 mg

MAKES 6 SERVINGS

1 ounce bacon, minced

½ cup diced onion

2 garlic cloves, minced

1 cup diced leek, white and light green parts

1 cup sliced carrot

1 cup sliced celeriac *or* salsify

1 cup sliced celery

2 tablespoons tomato paste

1 bay leaf

1 parsley sprig plus 1 tablespoon chopped

1 thyme sprig

1 garlic clove

3 to 4 black peppercorns

8 cups low-sodium chicken *or* vegetable broth

1½ cups dried French lentils

3 strips lemon peel

1 tablespoon white wine

1 tablespoon sherry vinegar

1 teaspoon kosher salt

¼ teaspoon freshly ground black pepper

1 tablespoon chopped chives

Cauliflower Almond Soup

Cauliflower and almond is a food match made in heaven. Using almond-cashew cream in place of regular heavy cream creates a rich soup without all the saturated fat. Almond-cashew cream is sold in the health food section of the grocery store.

1. Heat the almond oil in a large soup pot over medium heat. Add the celery and sweat until it begins to soften. Add the leek and continue to sweat until both vegetables are soft.

2. Steam a few cauliflower florets and set aside for garnish. Add the remaining cauliflower, the broth, salt, pepper, and nutmeg to the vegetable mixture and bring to a boil. Simmer until the cauliflower is soft, about 10 minutes.

3. Purée the soup in a blender or food processor. Stir in the almond-cashew cream. Serve each bowl of soup garnished with 1 tablespoon of the parsley, 2 tablespoons of the almonds, and a few of the reserved cauliflower florets.

Nutritional Information Per Serving: Calories 195, Protein 7 g, Carbohydrates 14 g, Fiber 4.5 g, Total Fat 14 g, Saturated Fat 1.5 g, Sodium 274 mg

MAKES 4 SERVINGS

2 tablespoons almond oil

2 stalks celery, chopped (about 1 cup)

1 leek, white and light green parts, sliced (about 1½ cups)

1 small head cauliflower separated into florets (about 4 cups)

1 quart low-sodium chicken broth

½ teaspoon kosher salt

¼ teaspoon freshly ground black pepper

¼ teaspoon ground nutmeg

¼ cup almond-cashew cream

¼ cup chopped parsley

½ cup sliced almonds, toasted

Cauliflower Almond Soup, served with
Roasted Kale and Blue Cheese Crisps
(page 21)

Lobster Corn Chowder

This soup is a twist on the traditional New England clam chowder and features two summery flavors: corn and lobster. Purchase eight ounces whole lobster with the shell to get the five ounces of meat that you'll need for this recipe.

1. Preheat the oven to 400°F.

2. Cover a baking sheet with parchment paper. Toss the corn with 1 teaspoon of the olive oil on the baking sheet. Roast the corn until it starts to brown, about 20 minutes. Set aside.

3. Heat the remaining 3 teaspoons oil in a large soup pot over medium heat. Add the green onion and sweat until tender, about 2 minutes.

4. Add the nonfat milk, broth, lobster shells, beans, thyme, Worcestershire, salt, and corn.

5. Whisk the evaporated nonfat milk and cornstarch together. Add to the soup and bring to a simmer. Continue to simmer until the soup is thickened, about 2 minutes.

6. Add the lobster meat and simmer until the lobster is cooked through, a few minutes more. Serve the soup garnished with the chives and parsley.

Nutritional Information Per Serving: Calories 213, Protein 15 g, Carbohydrates 28 g, Fiber 4 g, Total Fat 4.5 g, Saturated Fat 0.5 g, Sodium 313 mg

MAKES 6 SERVINGS

2 cups corn kernels

4 teaspoons olive oil

¾ cup thinly sliced green onions

2½ cups nonfat milk

2½ cups low-sodium chicken broth

5 ounces lobster tail meat, sliced, plus shells

1½ cups cooked "potato" beans, such as snow cap heirloom beans or calypso heirloom beans

1 thyme sprig

½ teaspoon Worcestershire sauce

½ teaspoon kosher salt

¾ cup evaporated nonfat milk

5 teaspoons cornstarch

1 tablespoon chopped chives

1 tablespoon chopped parsley

Wild Mushroom Soup

Puréeing this soup until it is very smooth gives the impression that it has cream in it because it is so luscious. You can also leave this hearty soup slightly chunky for a more rustic presentation.

1. Heat 2 tablespoons of the walnut oil in a medium soup pot over medium heat. Add the celeriac and celery and sweat until the vegetables begin to soften.

2. Add the shallot and all except 2 cups of the mushrooms and sweat until most of the liquid has evaporated and the vegetables are just beginning to brown.

3. Add 4 tablespoons of the white wine and allow to cook until most of the volume of the wine has reduced. Add the mushroom and chicken broths. Purée the mixture in a blender or food processor until smooth. Set aside and keep warm.

4. Heat the remaining 1 teaspoon walnut oil and sweat the reserved 2 cups mushrooms until most of their liquid has evaporated and they begin to brown.

5. Splash in the remaining 1 tablespoon white wine and reduce. Season with the salt and pepper. Return the puréed soup to the pot and stir in the some of the chives and parsley. Serve the soup garnished with the remaining chives, parsley, and a splash of sherry vinegar.

Nutritional Information Per Serving: Calories 140, Protein 4 g, Carbohydrates 11 g, Fiber 1.5 g, Total Fat 8.5 g, Saturated Fat 0.5 g, Sodium 220 mg

MAKES 4 SERVINGS

2 tablespoons plus 1 teaspoon walnut oil

½ cup diced celeriac

1 stalk celery, diced

1 large shallot, diced (about ⅓ cup)

12 ounces baby portobello mushrooms, sliced

5 tablespoons white wine

2 cups Wild Mushroom Broth (page 48)

1 cup low-sodium chicken broth

¼ teaspoon kosher salt

¼ teaspoons freshly ground black pepper

2 tablespoons chopped chives

¼ cup chopped parsley

1 tablespoon sherry vinegar

Chilled Beet and Fennel Soup

Roasting the beets and fennel brings out their natural sweetness. This is a refreshing soup to make for a hot, Indian summer day in September.

1. Preheat the oven to 400°F.

2. Roast the beets and fennel until the beets are tender and easily pierced with a fork, about 1 hour. Allow to cool until easy to handle. Run the beets under cold water and peel using your hands. Cut the beets into large pieces.

3. In a large soup pot, bring the beets, fennel, cabbage, garlic, ginger, and broth to a boil. Cover and simmer until the vegetables are tender, 35 to 40 minutes.

4. Remove the vegetables with a small amount of stock from the pot and purée in a blender or food processor until smooth. Strain the purée through a large-mesh sieve. Add the remaining stock back into the purée until it is the proper consistency. Season the soup with the salt, pepper, orange zest, and agave syrup. Chill the soup.

5. Serve the chilled soup with a dollop of yogurt and a fennel sprig.

Nutritional Information Per Serving: Calories 100, Protein 5 g, Carbohydrates 21.5 g, Fiber 5 g, Total Fat 0.5 g, Saturated Fat 0 g, Sodium 341 mg

MAKES 10 SERVINGS

3 pounds whole fresh beets

One 1-pound fennel bulb, cut in quarters

6 cups chopped savoy cabbage

2 garlic cloves, chopped

¼ cup chopped ginger

2 quarts vegetable broth

1 teaspoon kosher salt

¼ teaspoon freshly ground black pepper

1 teaspoon orange zest

1 tablespoon agave syrup

¾ cup nonfat Greek yogurt

6 fennel sprigs

Chilled Butternut Squash Soup

The fresh ginger adds a subtle bite to this refreshing, cold soup but still allows the squash flavor to come through. You can top each portion with an additional two tablespoons of nonfat, plain yogurt for an extra sixteen calories and two grams of carbohydrate. This soup is equally delicious served warm as a soup or a sauce, but you may want to use a pinch less of the white pepper since its flavor is more pronounced when warm.

2½ teaspoons minced ginger

2 tablespoons white wine

⅓ cup diced onion

½ cup diced celery

1 garlic clove, minced

3 cups chicken broth

7¼ cups peeled and cubed butternut squash

⅓ cup nonfat plain yogurt

3 tablespoons almond-cashew cream

1 teaspoon kosher salt

¼ teaspoon ground white pepper

2 tablespoons chopped chives

1. In a small pot, bring the ginger and wine to a simmer. Remove from heat and allow the ginger to steep for 30 minutes. Strain and discard the ginger.

2. In a large soup pot, sweat the onion, celery, and garlic in a small amount of the chicken broth until the onion is translucent, 4 to 5 minutes.

3. Add the remaining broth and the squash. Simmer until the squash is tender, 25 to 30 minutes. Purée the soup in a blender or food processor. Chill the soup.

4. Stir in the yogurt, almond-cashew cream, salt, pepper, and the ginger-infused wine. Serve the chilled soup with a sprinkling of chives.

Nutritional Information Per Serving: Calories 104, Protein 3.5 g, Carbohydrates 24 g, Fiber 4 g, Total Fat 1 g, Saturated Fat 0 g, Sodium 247 mg

Michigan-White Bean Soup

For a variation on this soup, eliminate the rosemary and balsamic vinegar. Garnish with nonfat plain yogurt and chives for the flavors of a baked potato.

1. Soak the beans for 8 to 24 hours in enough cold water to cover by 3 inches or refer to page 130 for the short soak method.

2. Drain the beans and simmer in the chicken broth until the beans are almost tender, about 30 minutes.

3. Meanwhile, in a medium sauté pan, cook the bacon until the fat renders and the bacon is crisp, 3 to 4 minutes. Add the leek, onion, garlic, salt, and pepper and sweat until the onions are translucent, 3 to 5 minutes.

4. Add the thyme, rosemary, bay leaves, and the onion mixture to the beans and simmer until the beans are completely tender, 15 to 20 minutes more. Remove the thyme, rosemary, and bay leaves.

5. Remove 1 cup of the beans with a little of the broth from the soup and purée in a blender or food processor. Stir the puréed beans back into the soup. Finish the soup by drizzling on the balsamic vinegar.

Nutritional Information Per Serving: Calories 177, Protein 10.5 g, Carbohydrates 27.5 g, Fiber 10 g, Total Fat 3 g, Saturated Fat 1 g, Sodium 174 mg

MAKES 8 SERVINGS

1¾ cups dried northern white beans

6 cups low-sodium chicken broth

1½ strips bacon, minced

¾ cup diced leek, white and light green parts

½ cup diced red onion

2 garlic cloves, minced

½ teaspoon kosher salt

¼ teaspoon freshly ground black pepper

1 thyme sprig

1 rosemary sprig

2 bay leaves

1 tablespoon balsamic vinegar

Cuban Black Bean Soup

Until I tried black bean soup with the lemon, sun-dried tomatoes, and sherry vinegar that this recipe uses, I was never crazy about it. Garnish it with some of the Mixed-Grain Pilaf *(page 179)* and wilted spinach and it becomes addictive.

1. Soak the beans for 8 to 12 hours in enough cold water to cover by 3 inches or refer to page 136 for the short soak method. Drain the beans and simmer in the chicken broth with the sachet until the beans are tender, 20 to 25 minutes. Remove the sachet.

2. In a large sauté pan, cook the bacon until the fat renders and the bacon begins to crisp. Add the canola oil. Add the onion, garlic, and cumin and sauté until the onion is translucent, 4 to 5 minutes.

3. Add the lemon, ancho and jalapeño chiles, tomatoes, oregano, salt, and onion mixture to the beans and simmer until the soup is flavorful, about 15 minutes more.

4. Remove and discard the lemon slices. Remove one-third of the beans from the soup and purée in a blender or food processor. Stir the puréed beans back into the soup. Stir in the vinegar.

5. In a small bowl, combine the cooked barley, rice, or pilaf and the spinach until well mixed. Serve each bowl of soup garnished with some of the rice mixture.

Nutritional Information Per Serving: Calories 298, Protein 18 g, Carbohydrates 51 g, Fiber 16 g, Total Fat 2.5 g, Saturated Fat 0.5 g, Sodium 386 mg

MAKES 6 SERVINGS

12 ounces dried black beans

8 cups low-sodium chicken broth

1 sachet d'épices (2 cloves, ⅛ teaspoon allspice, ⅛ teaspoon cumin seeds, and ¼ teaspoon black peppercorns)

½ ounce bacon, minced

1 teaspoon canola oil

¾ cup diced onion

2 garlic cloves, minced

¼ teaspoon ground cumin

1 lemon, thickly sliced

2 tablespoons toasted and chopped ancho chile

1 teaspoon minced jalapeño

¼ cup chopped sun-dried tomatoes

1 teaspoon oregano

1 teaspoon kosher salt

1 tablespoon sherry vinegar

¾ cup cooked barley, brown rice, *or* mixed-grain pilaf

½ cup wilted spinach, chopped

Cuban Black Bean Soup, served with
Chayote Salad with Oranges (page 164)

The Main Course

The answer to the question "What's for dinner?" is constantly evolving. Our current pattern of super-sized portions with animal protein at the center of the plate, accompanied by refined starches is not diabetes-friendly. It is time to redefine our dinner plates and rethink our approach to eating. This can be a challenging task. After all, it is called the "main" course and we are used to seeing a plate with large portions of meat or chicken. The healthy advice of filling only one-quarter of your plate with the protein can look meager to many and may encourage you to fill your plate with even less desirable refined starches. This is why so many enticing, vegetable-rich side dishes, salads, and soups are included in this book. They add a variety of tastes and textures to the meal so you can savor the smaller portions of protein and starches that you once used to gobble up and call a meal.

Impromptu Meal Planning

It is easier to create new meals if you have a little inspiration. Start by seeing what ingredients you have on hand in your home. If you keep your kitchen stocked with some of the foods suggested in chapter 1, it will be easier to create delicious, spur-of-the-moment meals. I look to world cuisines when creating new and health-enhancing recipes. Trying new cuisines keeps the pleasure and fun in cooking and planning meals. Often there are traditional dishes that put the emphasis on the better ingredients like the vegetables, grains, and beans and use the animal protein in smaller amounts. In addition, the flavor profiles have been perfected over generations so these healthful ingredients do not taste or look like diet food.

Regardless of the ingredients or techniques you use to make a meal, don't arrive in the kitchen or at the dinner table with a ravaging hunger. Your ability to plan and eat an appropriate meal and leave the table satisfied will be severely limited. Likewise don't arrive at the table with a buzz from alcohol. If you want to enjoy wine or alcohol, have it with your meal and double check with your physician about how alcohol will effect your diabetes management.

The following 5 steps can help you create satisfying, diabetes-friendly meals without a lot of advanced planning.

1. Select a lean protein (one-quarter of the plate)
2. Select non-starchy vegetables (half of the plate)
3. Select a whole grain, bean, or starch (one-quarter of the plate)
4. Select a flavor profile (see chart on page 71)
5. Choose a cooking technique based on protein selection (see the following description of techniques)

When half the foods that go into your meal are from non-starchy vegetables, you are off to a great start. In many cultures, vegetables are used to create sauces and condiments, such as a salsa. This is a great way to fit in vegetables without feeling like a rabbit in a garden chomping on fresh produce. See the list of the fifteen fabulous, flavorful, low-carbohydrate vegetables on page 130 for ideas.

The second half of your workspace will be shared by a lean source of protein such as fish, tofu, or poultry and a minimally processed grain or legume. Some of these grains and legumes can be cooked in large portions in advance and kept frozen in smaller quantities so they are ready to go into your meal in appropriate portions. See the chart on page 218 for cooking ratios and times for selected grains and a chart for cooking legumes on page 137.

Next you need to decide on a flavor profile and the best cooking techniques to match your ingredients. Your flavor profile can develop from your choice of aromatics, herbs, and spices you have on hand or you can plan in advance and try some of the flavor profiles from various world cuisines. The following table provides some flavor combinations from around the world. It is not a comprehensive list but rather a list of ingredients that are common and easy to keep on hand.

Table 4.1 Flavor Profile Table

Flavor Profile	Spices and Condiments	Aromatic Vegetables and Fresh Herbs	Oils and Acids
Japanese	Bonito flakes, dried kombu, soy sauce	Ginger, garlic, green onions	Rice wine, peanut oil
Thai	Fish sauce, soy sauce, coconut milk	Ginger, garlic, green onions, chiles, cilantro, lemongrass	Limes, rice vinegar, peanut oil
Chinese	Soy sauce, hoisin sauce, chiles, five-spice powder	Ginger, garlic, green onions	Sesame oil, rice vinegar
Mexican	Cilantro, dried chiles, cumin, oregano	Fresh chiles, garlic, onions, cilantro	Limes, tomatoes, avocados, canola oil
Mediterranean	Cumin, tapenade, paprika	Onions, garlic, fresh basil, parsley, mint	Olive oil, lemons, wine vinegar, yogurt
Indian	Cumin, coriander, cardamom, ginger, turmeric, chiles, black peppercorns	Onions, garlic, ginger, mint, cilantro	Yogurt, lemon, canola oil
French	Dijon mustard, thyme, bay leaves, tarragon, chervil	Shallots, leeks, celery, garlic, parsley, chives	Olive oil, butter, wine vinegars, lemon juice

Selecting a Cooking Technique

Several cooking techniques are used repeatedly in the preparation of the main course recipes in this book. Mastering these techniques, which is not hard to do, opens up a world of original cooking for you. You are no longer tied to having a recipe, buying the ingredients, and then cooking. You can pull together ingredients you already have on hand and use the appropriate cooking technique to make fabulous meals. Here are brief descriptions of the basic cooking techniques used throughout this book.

Grilling and Broiling

The dry, direct heat and quick cooking times associated with grilling are ideal for naturally tender portions of meat and poultry or firm cuts of fish. When grilling the heat source is below and when broiling it is from above.

- Trim meat and poultry of excess fat and, if needed, pound the pieces lightly to an even thickness.

- Fish may be left whole, with the skin on. Meatier fish, like swordfish, may be cut into steaks.

- Marinate high-protein foods before grilling and broiling to add flavor and reduce the development of potentially carcinogenic compounds on the surface.

- Start with the better-looking side of the meat or poultry facedown on the grill. Let it cook undisturbed on the first side until it is time to turn it. This develops better flavor and allows the meat or poultry to release naturally from the grill without sticking or tearing.

- To avoid burning the outer surface before the inside is cooked through, transfer the meat, chicken, or fish to the oven to finish cooking if necessary.

- Allow your food to cook partially before applying sauces and glazes to avoid burning them.

- Remove the meat, poultry, and fish when slightly underdone, as even thin pieces will retain some heat and continue to cook off the grill.

Sautéing/Pan Searing

This is a key technique to developing great flavor in meats and poultry or other firm types of protein. Season the protein with a dry spice rub or salt and pepper and make sure the surface of the protein is dry before it hits the hot pan.

- Use a heavy-gauge pan and a small amount of oil. The oil should be very hot before adding the food and allow each side to cook until very brown but not burned.

- Adjust the heat to help avoid burning, but do not reduce the heat too much or it will not develop a deep golden brown color.

- Once both sides have been seared, you can remove the protein and keep it warm if it is fully cooked or continue to cook it with some vegetables.

- As meats and poultry and even some seafood and vegetables are sautéed, their natural juices become concentrated in the drippings that cook down in the pan, forming what is referred to as the fond. This is very flavorful and should be deglazed from the bottom of the pan with water or broth to achieve the most flavor (see Deglazing on the facing page).

Sweating

Adding aromatic vegetables like onions and celery to the pan after sautéing and pan searing allows them to sweat and soften. Since very little fat, if any, is in the pan, you can splash in some broth, wine, or water to prevent the vegetables from burning.

- Do not add too much liquid to the pan to avoid steaming the vegetables.
- Start with the larger vegetables and add in the smaller aromatics like garlic once the larger vegetables have started to soften.

Deglazing

Adding a flavorful liquid to the pan after the seared/sautéed item is removed and the aromatic vegetables have softened dissolves the fond and allows the flavors to be recaptured in a sauce.

- Broth, wine, or juices can be used to deglaze a pan. Let the liquid reduce to a sauce-like consistency.
- Add a vegetable purée or a cornstarch slurry if desired, to help thicken the sauce.

Stir-frying

Like sautéing, stir-frying uses a small amount of oil over medium high heat to quickly cook food.

- Cut your meats and vegetables into smaller, uniform sizes so they cook quickly.
- Add foods in a sequence: Start with foods that require the longest cooking times and finish with those that cook in only a few moments at the end.

Braising and Stewing

These techniques are ideal for a number of tougher cuts of meat and poultry, making them tender over the course of a long cooking time. Brown the protein in a heavy-gauge pan with a lid that is just large enough to hold all the ingredients. Add the onions or other aromatic vegetable and allow them to cook until they are tender and the appropriate color, translucent for pale braises and stews or deep golden for brown braises and stews.

- For braises, add enough liquid to come one-third to one-half of the way up the side of the food.

- For stewing, the food is typically completely covered with liquid.

- Bring the liquid to just a simmer, not a full boil, to prevent toughening the meat. Adjust the heat as needed to maintain a slow simmer.

- Cover the pan tightly and finish cooking the braise or stew in a moderate oven or over low direct heat. You can also continue the cooking in a slow cooker and not worry about it getting overdone since the goal is often for the protein to become fork-tender and fall apart without a knife.

- When the protein is fork-tender, skim off any surface fat on the braising liquid and return it to a simmer. Cook any extra vegetables that will be served with the dish in this liquid before you add any thickener.

- Finally, thicken the sauce by boiling it to reduce its volume or adding a slurry of corn-starch or arrowroot dissolved in a small amount of water.

Shallow Poaching

By partially submerging poultry and fish in a liquid and placing it over gentle heat, you can combine steaming and simmering for quick yet delicate cooking. The benefit of shallow poaching is the flavorful pan sauce you can make from the poaching liquid as we did in the Fish Poached in Fennel-Orange Broth on page 94.

- When poaching poultry, remove the skin to avoid incorporating the fat into the cooking liquids that are usually served as part of the dish.

- Arrange individual servings of the poultry or fish in an oiled pan. Carefully add the cooking liquid of flavorful broth or wine, letting it come no higher than halfway up the food.

- Add aromatic ingredients such as herbs, spices, citrus zest, vegetables, vegetable juice, or wine to enhance the flavors of the dish.

- Place a round of parchment paper that just fits the pan over the food to capture some of the steam, then gently simmer and steam over low heat on the stovetop or in a moderate oven.

- Once the food is properly cooked, it can be removed from the pan and kept warm while you make a sauce from the remaining poaching liquid. Return the pan to high heat and let the poaching liquid boil until it is reduced by half. You can add minced herbs or other flavorings and thicken with a slurry of cornstarch or arrowroot if you desire.

Roasting

Since no fat needs to be added during cooking, roasting is a healthy cooking technique when used with larger cuts of meat and whole poultry or fish. Although most of the fat found in poultry is concentrated in the skin, leave the skin on when roasting poultry since it does not increase the fat in the meat of the bird. Also, do not remove the entire fat cap covering a meat roast. This will help the meat retain its natural juices. You can remove the skin from the chicken after it has finished roasting.

- Thoroughly degrease the pan drippings before using the fond as a sauce, if the skin or fat cap is left on while roasting.

- Herbs and other aromatics may also be placed under the skin of poultry to flavor the meat during cooking.

- Pat food dry before roasting to prevent it from steaming in its own moisture.

- Truss whole poultry or tie large roasts with string to give them a compact shape to encourage even cooking.

- Use a low-sided roasting pan and a rack to improve the circulation of hot air for even cooking. If you are roasting several large items, plan to leave several inches of space between them to allow hot air to circulate freely.

- The heat of the oven can dry out certain foods, especially those that require longer cooking times. Basting returns moisture to the food and imparts additional flavor. The fat and juices released by the food itself form the traditional basting liquid, but you can also baste with flavored oil or broth.

- If you will be preparing gravy from the pan drippings or want to roast vegetables to serve with the meal, add them to the roasting pan during the last 30 to 45 minutes of cooking time. Do not let these ingredients burn, or your gravy will taste bitter.

- Finally, allow a resting period before cutting and serving roasted meat or poultry. Resting allows the juices to redistribute evenly throughout the meat and the temperature to equalize, for better texture and flavor. Place in a warm spot, cover loosely with aluminum foil, and let sit for 5 to 20 minutes, depending on the size of the food.

Black Bean Cakes

The fiber and protein found in beans helps keep blood glucose levels from spiking too high after the meal. These cakes also make great hors d'oeuvre.

MAKES 4 SERVINGS

1 cup dried black beans

4 cups low-sodium chicken broth

¾ teaspoon kosher salt

½ ounce chopped Spanish-style chorizo sausage

⅓ cup diced onion

2 garlic cloves, minced

1 jalapeño, seeded and minced

½ teaspoon cumin seed, toasted and ground

½ teaspoon chili powder

1 egg white, lightly beaten

2 teaspoons fresh lime juice

1 tablespoon chopped cilantro

⅓ cup cornmeal

2 tablespoons olive oil

3 tablespoons nonfat Greek yogurt

¾ cup Tomato Salsa (page 77)

1. In a medium pot, soak the beans for 8 to 12 hours in enough cold water to cover by 3 inches or refer to page 136 for the quick soak method.

2. Drain the beans and simmer in the chicken broth with ½ teaspoon of the salt until tender, about 1 hour. Start to check doneness of the beans after 40 minutes. The beans should absorb almost all the broth. Add more broth if necessary.

3. In a medium sauté pan, cook the chorizo over low heat until the fat just begins to render, 5 to 8 minutes. Add the onion, garlic, and jalapeño and sauté until the onion start to brown. Add the cumin and chili powder and sauté until aromatic.

4. Mash the beans and combine with the egg white, lime juice, cilantro, the remaining ¼ teaspoon salt, and the chorizo mixture. Form the mixture into small cakes and lightly dust with the cornmeal.

5. Heat the olive oil in a large sauté pan over medium high heat. Sauté the cakes until golden brown on each side, 2 to 3 minutes. Keep warm.

6. Serve with the yogurt and tomato salsa.

Nutritional Information Per Serving: Calories 300, Protein 15.5 g, Carbohydrates 44 g, Fiber 13 g, Total Fat 8 g, Saturated Fat 1 g, Sodium 437 mg

Tomato Salsa

This semi-traditional take on tomato salsa can be customized by adding more jalapeño to make it spicier or more cilantro for a more pronounced herb flavor. These additions will have a negligible impact on the carbohydrate content of the dish.

Combine all the ingredients. Cover and chill for several hours, allowing the flavors to develop. Taste and adjust seasoning to taste.

Note Although fresh tomatoes are the best choice, good-quality, low-sodium, canned whole plum tomatoes may be substituted. The seeds and juice of the tomatoes may be reserved and used as a flavor enhancement in braised dishes.

Nutritional Information Per ¼ cup Serving: Calories 20, Protein 1 g, Carbohydrates 4 g, Fiber 0.5 g, Total Fat 0 g, Saturated Fat 0 g, Sodium 157 mg

MAKES 1 CUP

¾ cup peeled, seeded, and chopped tomato

½ jalapeño, seeded and minced

¼ cup minced red onion

¼ cup minced yellow bell pepper

1 tablespoon sliced green onion

1 tablespoon chopped cilantro

1 tablespoon fresh lime juice

¼ teaspoon freshly ground black pepper

¼ teaspoon kosher salt

Black Bean and Quinoa–Stuffed Zucchini

Quinoa makes a great base for stuffing vegetables; try using it with peppers, onions, or mushrooms. It is rich in protein and fiber, which means it digests more slowly, makes you feel full longer, and causes a more gradual rise in blood glucose levels.

1. Preheat the oven to 350°F.

2. Use a spoon to scoop about three-quarters of the flesh from the zucchini, reserving the flesh for another use such as making vegetable broth.

3. Transfer the zucchini to a baking sheet. Brush the zucchini with 4 teaspoons of the olive oil and season with ½ teaspoon of the salt and the pepper.

4. Heat the remaining 1 teaspoon olive oil in medium sauce pan. Sweat the onion, celery, and jalapeño until soft. Add the quinoa, cumin, coriander, and the remaining ¼ teaspoon salt. Toast briefly but do not allow the mixture to burn. Add the vegetable stock and bring to a boil. Reduce the heat, cover, and simmer until the quinoa is soft and the liquid is absorbed, about 15 minutes.

5. Combine the cooked quinoa, beans, cheese, cilantro, marjoram, and oregano.

6. Spoon the mixture into the hollowed cavity of the zucchini, pressing to make sure it stays in place.

7. Bake until the zucchini is tender, 15 to 20 minutes.

Nutritional Information Per Serving: Calories 289, Protein 17 g, Carbohydrates 37 g, Fiber 9 g, Total Fat 9.5 g, Saturated Fat 2 g, Sodium 459 mg

MAKES 4 SERVINGS

4 large zucchinis, halved lengthwise

5 teaspoons olive oil

¾ teaspoon kosher salt

¼ teaspoon freshly ground black pepper

¼ diced small onion

¼ cup diced celery

½ jalapeño, seeded and minced

½ cup quinoa

½ teaspoon ground cumin

½ teaspoon ground coriander

1 cup vegetable broth

1 cup cooked black beans

¾ cup grated Cheddar

1 tablespoon chopped cilantro

1 tablespoon chopped marjoram

2 teaspoons chopped oregano

Grilled Tofu with Eggplant and Parmesan

The secret to grilling tofu is to first press it until most of its moisture comes out. I layer it between paper towels while pressing it and change the towels as they get wet. The smokiness from grilling eggplant and tofu adds a nice twist to the flavors of eggplant Parmesan.

1. Press the blocks of tofu between paper towels for at least 30 minutes to remove the excess water. Slice each block of tofu lengthwise into three pieces and then slice each block in half.

2. Sprinkle eggplant slices with the salt and allow to sit for 30 minutes. Rinse eggplant well and reserve eight slices. Cut the remaining slices into ½-inch cubes.

3. To prepare the marinade, dissolve the arrowroot in 1 tablespoon of the chicken broth and set aside. Bring the remaining chicken broth to a boil and stir in the dissolved arrowroot. Allow to boil until it thickens slightly. Stir in the remaining marinade ingredients and 1 tablespoon of the chopped basil.

4. Add the tofu and eggplant slices to the marinade and leave for at least 30 minutes.

5. Heat the olive oil in a sauté pan over medium heat. Add the green pepper, onion, and garlic and sauté until they start to soften, 2 to 3 minutes. Add the eggplant cubes and cook until soft, an additional 2 to 3 minutes. Add the tomato sauce and ¼ teaspoon Italian seasoning and allow to simmer while you grill the tofu and eggplant.

6. Heat a nonstick or cast-iron grill pan over high heat. Remove the tofu and eggplant slices from the marinade and heat the remaining marinade in a small saucepan. Place the tofu and eggplant in the pan and grill until grill marks form and both sides are lightly browned.

MAKES 4 SERVINGS

Two 14-ounce packages extra-firm tofu (do not use silken tofu)

1 large eggplant, peeled and cut into ½-inch-thick slices

1 teaspoon kosher salt

1 tablespoon olive oil

1 green bell pepper, diced

1 small onion, diced

2 garlic cloves, diced

2 cups tomato sauce (low-sodium jarred or homemade)

1¼ teaspoons Italian seasoning

6 tablespoons chopped basil

2 ounces grated Parmesan

RED WINE MARINADE

¾ teaspoon arrowroot

¾ cup chicken broth

¼ cup red wine vinegar

¼ cup olive oil

¼ teaspoon kosher salt (omit if using a canned broth)

¼ teaspoon freshly ground black pepper

3 garlic cloves, minced

Place the tofu in between two absorbent towels in between two cutting boards, and weigh it down with a heavy object to remove excess moisture.

7. Alternately layer 3 slices of grilled tofu and 2 slices of eggplant with a little Parmesan and chopped basil between each layer. Top with the eggplant tomato sauce and garnish with remaining Parmesan and basil.

Nutritional Information Per Serving: Calories 426, Protein 28 g, Carbohydrates 29 g, Fiber 11 g, Total Fat 22 g, Saturated Fat 5 g, Sodium 373 mg

Tofu with Red Curry Paste, Peas, Green Onions, and Cilantro

Pressing the tofu between paper towels *(see photo page 80)* helps remove excess moisture so the tofu cubes develop a crispy, browned exterior. However, if you are in a hurry, it is not essential to the great flavor of this dish. Consider serving this dish with chickpeas mashed with chicken or vegetable broth and peanuts in place of the traditional rice accompaniment.

1. Heat the peanut oil in a skillet over medium high heat. Add the tofu cubes and cook until they are golden on all sides, 5 to 7 minutes. To help the tofu cubes maintain their shape, turn them with a flat spatula. Remove from the skillet and sprinkle with the lime juice.

2. Add the carrot and onion to the skillet and sweat until soft, 4 to 5 minutes. Add the garlic and cook until fragrant, about 1 minute more. Splash the vegetables with a small amount of chicken or vegetable broth to prevent them from sticking to the bottom of the skillet and burning. Add the tomatoes and green peas and sweat just until they release a little of their liquid.

3. Stir in the curry paste, turmeric, salt, and pepper. Add the coconut milk, reduce the heat, and simmer until the sauce has thickened slightly, 6 to 8 minutes.

4. Stir the tofu cubes back into the pan and heat through. Stir in the cilantro, green onion, and peanuts.

Nutritional Information Per Serving: Calories 238, Protein 8 g, Carbohydrates 14 g, Fiber 5 g, Total Fat 18 g, Saturated Fat 4.5 g, Sodium 380 mg

MAKES 4 SERVINGS

1½ tablespoons peanut oil

½ package (8 ounces) extra-firm tofu, drained and pressed to remove moisture and cut into cubes

1 tablespoon fresh lime juice

1 medium carrot, peeled and diced

¼ cup diced onion

2 garlic cloves, minced

Chicken *or* Vegetable Broth (page 44 or 47) as needed for sweating vegetables

1 cup grape tomatoes, halved

½ cup frozen green peas, thawed

2 tablespoons red curry paste

¼ teaspoon ground turmeric

¼ teaspoon kosher salt

¼ teaspoon freshly ground black pepper

¾ cup light coconut milk

¼ cup chopped cilantro

¼ cup minced green onions

¼ cup chopped peanuts

Taco Salad with Tempeh

Tempeh has a neutral flavor that takes on the spicy taco seasoning. Fermented from soybeans, and sometimes other grains as well, it is firmer than tofu and crumbles and browns well, like ground turkey or beef. However, tempeh has no cholesterol and is low in saturated fat.

MAKES 4 SERVINGS

1. Preheat the oven to 350°F.

2. Bake the corn tortilla strips until lightly brown and crispy, about 25 minutes. Set aside.

3. Juice half the lime. Whisk in 1 tablespoon of the canola oil and ¼ teaspoon of the taco seasoning. Set aside.

4. Heat the 2 teaspoons remaining canola oil in a skillet. Add the tempeh and cook until browned. Add the green and red peppers and onion and sweat until the vegetables begin to soften. Add the jalapeño, garlic, and the remaining taco seasoning and continue to sweat until the vegetables soft. Splash in some of the liquid from the canned tomatoes if ingredients are starting to stick to the bottom of the pan.

5. Once the vegetables are completely soft, add the tomatoes, the water, tomato paste, brown sugar, and salt.

6. Simmer, allowing the flavors to blend, 15 to 20 minutes. Stir in 1 cup of the cilantro. Toss the mixed greens with the reserved dressing and top with tempeh mixture, toasted tortilla strips, shredded cheese, and the remaining cilantro.

Nutritional Information Per Serving: Calories 363, Protein 19 g, Carbohydrates 31 g, Fiber 5 g, Total Fat 20.5 g, Saturated Fat 6.25 g, Sodium 443 mg

Three 6-inch diameter corn tortillas, cut into ⅛-inch strips

1 lime, cut in half

1 tablespoon plus 2 teaspoons canola oil

2¾ tablespoons Dry Taco Seasoning (page 86)

One 8-ounce package three-grain tempeh, cut into ¼-inch dice

½ green bell pepper, chopped (about ½ cup)

½ red bell pepper, chopped (about ½ cup)

½ onion, chopped (about ½ cup)

1 small jalapeño, minced

1 garlic clove, minced (about 1 teaspoon)

One 14.5-ounce can no-added-salt diced tomatoes

½ cup water

1 tablespoon tomato paste

2 teaspoons brown sugar

½ teaspoon kosher salt

1½ cups cilantro leaves, chopped

6 cups mixed greens such as frisée and Bibb lettuce

3 ounces sharp Cheddar, shredded

Dry Taco Seasoning

Keep this taco seasoning on hand for whenever you want to spice up some ground meat or sautéed vegetables for a wrap. It is lower in sodium than most packaged taco seasonings. Epazote is an herb used in Mexican cooking. It is similar to oregano, so you can increase the oregano in the mix if epazote is not avilable.

Mix all the ingredients together and store in an airtight container.

Nutritional Information Per 1 Tablespoon Serving: Calories 21, Protein 0.5 g, Carbohydrates 4 g, Fiber 1 g, Total Fat 0.5 g, Saturated Fat 0 g, Sodium 219 mg

¾ teaspoon kosher salt

1 teaspoon onion powder

1 teaspoon paprika

1 teaspoon sugar

¼ teaspoon ground chipotle pepper

¼ teaspoon cayenne

1 tablespoon ground cumin

1 tablespoon dried cilantro, crushed

1 teaspoon dried epazote

1 teaspoon oregano (preferably Mexican)

1 teaspoon garlic powder

½ teaspoon freshly ground black pepper

Shrimp in Yogurt Curry Sauce

This dish tastes great when served over spinach sautéed in a little garlic and oil in place of a starch. This will keep the carbohydrate content of the meal lower. Silken tofu can be used in place of the nonfat sour cream if desired.

1. Heat the olive oil in a saucepan over medium heat. Add the celery and onion and sweat until soft. Add the garlic and curry powder and sweat until the garlic is soft.

2. Stir in the apple and lime juice. Add the yogurt, sour cream, bay leaf, salt, pepper, and shrimp. Simmer gently until the shrimp is cooked through, about 3 minutes.

3. Stir in the cilantro and green onion and serve.

Nutritional Information Per Serving (not including side dishes): Calories 205, Protein 26 g, Carbohydrates 13 g, Fiber 1 g, Total Fat 5 g, Saturated Fat 1 g, Sodium 352 mg

MAKES 4 SERVINGS

2 teaspoons olive oil

2 tablespoons finely chopped celery

¼ cup finely chopped onion

1 teaspoon finely minced garlic

3 teaspoons curry powder (Rogan Josh-Style is particularly nice)

½ Granny Smith apple, peeled and cut into ¼-inch cubes

1 teaspoon fresh lime juice

½ cup nonfat yogurt

½ cup nonfat sour cream

½ bay leaf

½ teaspoon kosher salt

¼ teaspoon freshly ground black pepper

1 pound large shrimp, peeled and deveined

1 tablespoon chopped cilantro

1 tablespoon sliced green onion

Seared Scallops with Beet Vinaigrette

This entrée is low in calories, carbohydrates, and fat so it is a great meal to have before heading out to a party where you plan to indulge a little.

1. Place the beets in a large saucepot and cover with two inches of water. Add ½ tablespoon of the cider vinegar, bring to a boil, reduce the heat and simmer until tender, 12 to 15 minutes. Drain them well. When the beets are cool enough to handle, slip off the skins using a towel and chop. Purée the chopped beets and the remaining 1 tablespoon cider vinegar in a blender or food processor until smooth. Whisk in the olive oil and season with the dill, salt, and pepper. Set aside.

2. Dry the scallops with paper towels. Heat the canola oil in a skillet over medium high heat. Sear the scallops until browned on both sides and cooked through, about 2 minutes per side. Toss the greens, carrots, and daikon radish with some of beet vinaigrette. Arrange the scallops with the greens and vegetables and drizzle remaining beet vinaigrette around scallops.

Note For a more intense color and flavor, use a juice machine to juice the raw beets. Combine the juice and vinegar, whisk in the oil, and season with dill, salt, and pepper.

Nutritional Information Per Serving: Calories 208, Protein 25 g, Carbohydrates 9 g, Fiber 1.5 g, Total Fat 8 g, Saturated Fat 1 g, Sodium 402 mg

MAKES 4 SERVINGS

4 ounces whole fresh beets

3 tablespoons cider vinegar

1½ tablespoons extra-virgin olive oil

1 teaspoon chopped dill

½ teaspoon kosher salt

⅛ teaspoon freshly ground black pepper

1 pound 4 ounces sea scallops, muscle tabs removed

1 teaspoon canola oil

4 cups mixed greens

⅓ cup julienned carrot

⅓ cup julienned daikon radish

Almond-Crusted Baked Scallops

This dish is comfort food with the health benefits of seafood and almonds. Consider serving with arugula tossed with Mustard-Sherry Vinaigrette *(page 175)*.

(page 175)

1. Preheat the oven to 400°F.

2. Combine the yogurt, mustard, ¼ teaspoon of the paprika, ¼ teaspoon of the salt, and the pepper. Coat the scallops with the yogurt mixture and chill while preparing the almond coating.

3. Combine the almonds, bread crumbs, the remaining 1 teaspoon paprika, and the remaining ½ teaspoon salt. Toss the yogurt-coated scallops with the almond bread crumb mixture and place in a greased baking dish. Bake until the coating is golden and internal temperature of scallops registers 145°F on an instant-read thermometer, 15 to 20 minutes.

Nutritional Information Per Serving: Calories 284, Protein 27 g, Carbohydrates 16 g, Fiber 3 g, Total Fat 13 g, Saturated Fat 1 g, Sodium 462 mg

MAKES 6 SERVINGS

6 tablespoons nonfat Greek yogurt

1 tablespoon Dijon mustard

1¼ teaspoons smoked Spanish paprika

¾ teaspoon kosher salt

¼ teaspoon freshly ground black pepper

1 pound 8 ounces scallops, muscle tabs removed

1 cup whole almonds, toasted and ground into a course meal

½ cup plain bread crumbs

Salmon Poached in Coconut Milk

Jasmine rice may seem like an obvious choice with this dish but try steamed barley instead. Barley pairs well with the sauce and it has a lower glycemic impact and more fiber than rice. Steamed, julienned snow peas are a great accompaniment and a dry, tart, medium-bodied white wine like Sauvignon Blanc would make this a special meal.

1. Preheat the oven to 350°F. Cut a piece of parchment paper the size of the pan being used to poach the fish.

2. Heat the peanut oil in a shallow ovenproof pan over medium high heat. Add the shallots, garlic, ginger, cubanelle chile, and lime zest and sweat until soft. Add the broth, coconut milk, and lemongrass, if using.

3. Season the salmon with the salt and pepper and add any remaining salt to the poaching liquid in the pan. Place the salmon in the poaching liquid and cover with the piece of parchment paper.

4. Place the pan in the oven and poach just until the fillets are opaque, about 7 minutes. Remove the fish from the poaching liquid and cover to keep warm. Strain the poaching liquid and reduce it to a thin sauce consistency. Stir in the green onion and cilantro and serve over the fish.

Nutritional Information Per Serving: Calories 317, Protein 25 g, Carbohydrates 6 g, Fiber 0 g, Total Fat 21 g, Saturated Fat 7 g, Sodium 282 mg

MAKES 4 SERVINGS

2 teaspoons peanut oil

¼ cup minced shallots (about 2 shallots)

2 tablespoons minced garlic (about 4 cloves)

2 tablespoons minced ginger

2 tablespoons minced cubanelle chile or other mild chile

½ teaspoon lime zest

1½ cups low-sodium chicken broth

1 cup light coconut milk

One 4-inch piece lemongrass, minced *(optional)*

1 to 1 pound 8 ounces salmon fillets

½ teaspoon kosher salt

¼ teaspoon freshly ground black pepper

1 tablespoon chopped green onion

1 tablespoon minced cilantro

Multigrain Pasta with Broccolini, Crab Meat, and Orange, Sesame, and Ginger Dressing

Experiment with different brands of multigrain pastas to find one that appeals to you. Be sure that the multigrain pasta contains whole grains so it will be high in fiber.

1. Warm the sesame oil in a small saucepan and stir in the orange zest. Set aside.

2. Mix the arrowroot and 1 teaspoon of broth together to form a paste.

3. Bring the remaining broth to a boil. Add the soy sauce and arrowroot paste. Allow the broth to boil until thickened slightly, stirring constantly.

4. Remove from the heat and add the orange juice, ¼ teaspoon of the salt, and the black pepper and whisk in the sesame oil mixture. Keep the dressing warm.

5. Cook the pasta in boiling water with the remaining ½ teaspoon salt until al dente. Drain and toss with the crab meat and half the dressing.

6. Heat the peanut oil in a sauté pan over medium heat. Add the ginger, garlic, and green onion and sauté until fragrant. Add the broccolini and red pepper and sauté until soft. Add the pasta mixture and the remaining dressing and toss to coat the pasta evenly. Garnish with the sesame seeds.

Nutritional Information Per Serving: Calories 464, Protein 28 g, Carbohydrates 53 g, Fiber 7 g, Total Fat 15 g, Saturated Fat 2 g, Sodium 621 mg

MAKES 4 SERVINGS

1 tablespoon pure sesame oil

3 teaspoons orange zest

1 teaspoon arrowroot

1 cup low-sodium chicken broth

1 tablespoon reduced-sodium soy sauce

⅓ cup fresh orange juice

¾ teaspoon kosher salt

½ teaspoon freshly ground black pepper

8 ounces whole grain spaghetti

1¼ cups cooked crab meat

2 tablespoons peanut oil

1½ tablespoons minced ginger

1½ tablespoons minced garlic

¼ cup finely chopped green onions

1 bunch baby broccolini, sliced on the diagonal (about 2 cups), blanched

1 large red bell pepper, sliced

4 teaspoons sesame seeds, toasted

Fish Poached in Fennel-Orange Broth

This shallow poaching technique can be used for most any type of fish and with a variety of flavor profiles. If you double the recipe for more portions, be sure to increase the size of the pan. The flavorful poaching liquid becomes a delicious sauce to serve over the fish.

MAKES 4 SERVINGS

4 teaspoons almond oil

1 pound 8 ounces fish fillet, such as flounder or salmon

½ teaspoon kosher salt

½ teaspoon freshly ground black pepper

2 cups thinly sliced fennel bulb

2 cups sliced leek, white and light green parts

2 garlic cloves, thinly sliced

1 teaspoon orange zest

3 cups low-sodium chicken broth

1 orange, juiced

2 teaspoons arrowroot

¼ cup toasted sliced almonds

¼ cup minced fennel fronds

1. Preheat oven to 350°F. Cut a piece of parchment paper the size of the pan being used to poach the fish. Coat the parchment paper with a thin layer of the almond oil.

2. Season the fish with the salt and pepper and set aside. Heat the remaining almond oil in the pan over medium heat. Add the fennel and sweat until it starts to soften. Add the leek, garlic, and orange zest. Once the leeks begin to soften, place the fish fillet on top of the vegetables.

3. Add enough of the broth to come half to three-quarters of the way up the sides of the fish. Add the orange juice and cover with the prepared parchment paper, oiled side down. Place the pan in the oven and poach just until the fish is opaque, 10 to 15 minutes.

4. Remove the fish from the pan and cover to keep warm. Strain the poaching liquid into a small saucepan and reserve the vegetables. Mix the arrowroot with 1 tablespoon water to form a paste. Bring the poaching liquid to a boil and add the arrowroot paste.

Gently place the fish in the poaching liquid, taking care that the level of the liquid only comes halfway of the way up the fish.

Place the parchment paper on top of the fish while it cooks.

The finished fish will be opaque and relatively firm to the touch.

5. Allow to boil until the volume of the poaching liquid is reduced by half and thickened to a sauce consistency. Stir in the almonds and fennel fronds and serve with the sauce poured over the fish and vegetables.

Nutritional Information Per Serving: Calories 491, Protein 39 g, Carbohydrates 14 g, Fiber 3 g, Total Fat 30 g, Saturated Fat 6 g, Sodium 324 mg

Salmon and Wild Rice–Stuffed
Cabbage, served with Edamame with
Tarragon Dipping Sauce (page 166)

Salmon and Wild Rice–Stuffed Cabbage

These cabbage rolls will be enjoyed by seafood lovers and non-seafood lovers alike. Keep some cooked wild rice in the freezer in small portions so it is available to add into dishes such as this one. You can also use rinsed, canned salmon in place of the fresh salmon.

1. Preheat the oven to 350°F.

2. Bring the water to a boil and remove from the heat. Steep the dried mushrooms for 10 minutes. Strain the mushrooms and reserve the steeping liquid. Chop the mushrooms and set aside.

3. Add enough water to the reserved mushroom liquid to make 1 cup. Add ⅛ teaspoon of the salt and bring it to a boil. Stir in the barley and reduce the heat to a simmer. Cover and cook until the barley is soft, about 25 minutes.

4. Stir the chopped soaked mushrooms into the barley. Mix the cooked barley with the wild rice and set aside.

5. Heat the olive oil in a heavy skillet over medium high heat. Season the salmon fillet with ⅛ teaspoon each salt and pepper. Sear the salmon fillet just until cooked, about 2 minutes per side. Remove the skin from the salmon if still on and flake the fish into the barley mixture. Brown the fresh mushrooms in the same pan. Remove the mushrooms and deglaze the pan with ¼ cup of the wine.

6. Add the skillet liquids and mushrooms to the barley mixture. Add the green onions, tarragon, the remaining ½ teaspoon salt, pepper, and the lemon zest.

7. Fill the cabbage leaves with the barley mixture and roll the leaves up tightly. Place the rolls seam side down in a baking dish.

8. Bring the chicken broth and the remaining ¼ cup wine to a boil and pour over the cabbage rolls. Cover with foil and bake until cabbage is soft and the broth is steaming, 20 to 25 minutes.

Nutritional Information Per Serving: Calories 384, Protein 24 g, Carbohydrates 24 g, Fiber 8 g, Total Fat 15 g, Saturated Fat 3 g, Sodium 326 mg

MAKES 4 SERVINGS

1 cup water

½ cup dried shiitake or porcini mushrooms

¾ teaspoon kosher salt

½ cup pearled barley

¾ cup cooked wild rice

2 teaspoons olive oil

12 ounces salmon fillet

¼ teaspoon freshly ground black pepper, plus more as needed

8 ounces sliced fresh shiitake mushrooms

½ cup white wine

¾ cup chopped green onions

1¼ teaspoons dried tarragon

1½ teaspoons lemon zest

8 large cabbage leaves, blanched

½ cup low-sodium chicken broth

Halibut with Summer Vegetables

The fresh summer flavors of this dish blend nicely with the earthiness of the Mushroom-Parmesan Salad *(page 155).*

1. Preheat the oven to 375°F.

2. Toss the zucchini, squash, tomatoes, onion, garlic, basil, oregano, and 1 tablespoon of the olive oil. Spread in a thin, even layer in a 9 by 13-inch baking dish. Place in the oven while preparing the fish.

3. Season the fish with the salt and pepper. Heat the remaining 2 teaspoons olive oil in a large skillet over high heat. Add the fillets and sear until golden brown, 1 to 2 minutes per side. Squeeze the half lemon over the fish.

4. Place the fillets and their juices on top of the vegetables, pouring the cooking juices over all. Continue to roast until the fish is cooked through, 5 to 10 minutes. Serve each fillet over a bed of the vegetables.

Nutritional Information Per Serving: Calories 267, Protein 37 g, Carbohydrates 7 g, Fiber 2 g, Total Fat 10 g, Saturated Fat 1.5 g, Sodium 167 mg

MAKES 4 SERVINGS

1 medium zucchini, sliced into ¼-inch rounds

1 yellow summer squash, sliced into ¼-inch rounds

3 plum tomatoes, peeled, seeded, and cut into large dice

½ yellow onion, diced

2 garlic cloves, sliced

1 tablespoon minced basil

½ teaspoon minced oregano

1 tablespoon plus 2 teaspoons olive oil

4 halibut fillets (about 6 ounces each)

¼ teaspoon kosher salt

¼ teaspoon freshly ground black pepper

½ lemon

Halibut with Summer Vegetables served
with Mushroom-Parmesan Salad (page 155)

Tilapia with Grapefruit Salsa, served with
Sugar Snap Peas with Champagne Vinaigrette
(page 160) and Black-eyed Pea Salad (page 176)

Tilapia with Grapefruit Salsa

The individual quick-frozen tilapia fillets are a great convenience and a quality product. You can also substitute canned grapefruit sections and canned mandarin oranges packed in juice if fresh citrus is not available. However, in-season citrus will almost always taste a little better.

MAKES 4 SERVINGS

6 tilapia fillets (about 6 ounces each)

¼ teaspoon kosher salt

⅛ teaspoon freshly ground black pepper

1½ tablespoons olive oil

Grapefruit Salsa (page 101)

1. Season the fillets with the salt and pepper.

2. Heat the olive oil in a sauté pan over medium high heat. Add the fillets and cook on each side until golden brown and cooked through, 2 to 3 minutes. Serve with the grapefruit salsa.

Nutritional Information Per Serving: Calories 193, Protein 34 g, Carbohydrates 0 g, Fiber 0 g, Total Fat 6.5 g, Saturated Fat 1.5 g, Sodium 135 mg

Grapefruit Salsa

The spiciness of the habanero pairs well with the cool grapefruit and is tempered by the refreshing flavor of cilantro. This salsa pairs well with pork and chicken as well as fish.

MAKES 6 SERVINGS

2 Ruby Red grapefruits (about 1 cup sections)

1 navel orange (about ½ cup sections)

2 tablespoons chopped cilantro

¼ cup minced red onion

1 teaspoon minced habanero pepper

1 tablespoon chopped parsley

½ teaspoon kosher salt

¼ teaspoon freshly ground black pepper

1. Cut the peel and pith off the grapefruits and orange. Cut on both sides of the membranes to release each citrus section.

2. Combine the grapefruit and orange sections with the cilantro, onion, habanero, parsley, salt, and pepper. Toss carefully so as not to break the citrus sections.

Nutritional Information Per 5 Tablespoon Serving: Calories 56, Protein 1 g, Carbohydrates 14 g, Fiber 2 g, Total Fat 0 g, Saturated Fat 0 g, Sodium 94 mg

Chicken Breast Fillet with Moroccan Tomato Sauce

The cinnamon and ginger in the sauce hints of sweetness while the chipotle chile balances it with a little bit of heat. Try making this dish during the middle of summer when sweet, ripe-off-the-vine tomatoes are available for an added burst of flavor.

1. Trim the chicken breast of excess fat. Pull away the tender from the underside of each breast and reserve for another use. Make a cut through the thickest part of breast to butterfly it and pound to an even thickness of about ¼ inch. Mix the flour, cinnamon, ginger, salt, black pepper, and chipotle chile powder.

2. Dredge the chicken in the flour mixture. Heat the olive oil in a heavy skillet over medium high heat. Sear each breast, about 2 minutes per side.

3. Set the chicken aside and keep warm. Add the garlic to the pan cook until soft. Deglaze the pan with the white wine and broth.

4. Mix the arrowroot with 1 tablespoon water to form a paste. Reduce the volume of the wine mixture by half and thicken with the arrowroot paste. Stir in the tomatoes and simmer for 10 minutes.

5. Return the chicken to the pan and heat through. Serve with the sauce spooned over the chicken. Garnish with the cilantro and sesame seeds.

Nutritional Information Per Serving: Calories 274, Protein 25.5 g, Carbohydrates 11 g, Fiber 1 g, Total Fat 12 g, Saturated Fat 2 g, Sodium 219 mg

MAKES 4 SERVINGS

1 pound boneless, skinless chicken breast

1 tablespoon flour

½ teaspoon ground cinnamon

½ teaspoon ground ginger

½ teaspoon kosher salt

½ teaspoon freshly ground black pepper

Pinch ground chipotle chile powder

2 tablespoons olive oil

2 garlic cloves, minced

½ cup dry white wine

¾ cup low-sodium chicken broth

¼ teaspoon arrowroot

2 large tomatoes, seeded and diced or one 14.5-ounce can low-sodium diced tomatoes

1½ tablespoons chopped cilantro

1½ tablespoons sesame seeds, toasted

OPPOSITE: Chicken Breast Fillet with Moroccan Tomato Sauce, served with Barley and Couscous Pilaf (page 178)

Chicken Kebabs with Mint-Parsley Pesto,
served with Mixed-Grain Pilaf (page 179)
and Cucumber, Onion, and Parsley Salad
with Feta (page 144)

Chicken Kebabs with Mint-Parsley Pesto

These kebabs are excellent served with a Mixed-Grain Pilaf *(page 179)* or the Barley and Couscous Pilaf *(page 178)* and the Cucumber, Onion, and Parsley Salad with Feta *(page 144)*.

1. Cut the chicken breast into 1-inch cubes. Be sure the cubes are similarly sized so the chicken cooks evenly.

2. Set aside 1½ tablespoons of the pesto. Place the chicken on skewers and marinate in the remaining pesto for at least 1 hour.

3. Grill the chicken until the thickest piece registers 165°F on a meat thermometer but be cautious not to overcook the chicken or it will be tough and dry. Sprinkle with the salt and drizzle with the reserved pesto before serving.

Nutritional Information Per Serving: Calories 279, Protein 24 g, Carbohydrates 1.5 g, Fiber 0.5 g, Total Fat 20 g, Saturated Fat 3 g, Sodium 180 mg

MAKES 4 SERVINGS

2 boneless, skinless chicken breasts

½ cup Mint-Parsley Pesto (page 34)

¼ teaspoon kosher salt

4 bamboo skewers

Lemon-Parsley Chicken Breasts

Try this dish with the Quinoa and Nut-Stuffed Portobello Mushroom (page 31) as a side. You can also use skewered shrimp in place of chicken and cook for only 2 minutes per side.

1. Preheat the oven to 350°F.

2. Pound the thickest part of the chicken breasts between plastic wrap until the breasts are an even ½ inch thickness. Cut the chicken into 4 portions and marinate the chicken in the vinaigrette for 30 minutes.

3. Heat a grill pan and coat with canola oil. Remove the chicken from the vinaigrette and reserve the vinaigrette. Season the chicken with salt and pepper.

4. Grill the breasts for about 2 minutes per side, or until they have grill marks, while brushing with vinaigrette. Continue cooking in the oven until the thickest part of the breast registers 165°F on a meat thermometer, about 10 minutes.

MAKES 4 SERVINGS

1 pound 8 ounces boneless, skinless chicken breasts (about 2 large breasts)

½ teaspoon kosher salt

½ teaspoon black pepper

1 teaspoon canola oil

½ cup Lemon Parsley Vinaigrette (page 106)

Lemon-Parsley Vinaigrette

Lemon and parsley combine here for a versatile vinaigrette that can be used as a dressing for a grain salad or marinade for grilled meats and vegetables. Lemon pairs well with a variety of herbs, so you can substitute with whatever you find at your local farmstand.

1. Combine the lemon juice, vinegar, mustard, garlic, shallot, salt, pepper, fennel seeds, and cayenne.

2. Whisk in the oil and set aside.

3. Whisk in the parsley and oregano just before using the vinaigrette.

Note For each ¼ cup of vinaigrette add about 2 teaspoons chopped parsley leaves and 1 teaspoon chopped oregano leaves. The remaining vinaigrette, without added herbs can be stored in the refrigerator and used as needed with the fresh herbs added just before using.

Nutrition Information Per Tablespoon: Calories 73, Protein 0 g, Carbohydrates 1 g, Fiber 0 g, Total Fat 8 g, Saturated Fat 1 g, Sodium 64 mg

MAKES 1⅓ CUPS

6 tablespoons fresh lemon juice

2 tablespoons Pinot Grigio or champagne vinegar

1½ teaspoons Dijon mustard

2 garlic cloves, minced (about 1½ teaspoons)

½ shallot, minced (about 1 tablespoon)

1 teaspoon kosher salt

½ teaspoon freshly ground black pepper

2 teaspoons fennel seeds, crushed

¼ teaspoon cayenne

¾ cup olive oil

¾ cup minced parsley leaves

2 tablespoons minced oregano

Lemon-Parsley Chicken Breasts, served with Quinoa and
Nut–Stuffed Portobello Mushroom (page 31)

Chicken, Quinoa, and Parsley Salad

Quinoa is a whole grain that is rich in complete protein. It is available in different colors. I like to use the red quinoa because the color contrasts beautifully with the chicken and parsley.

MAKES 6 SERVINGS

¼ cup plus 1 tablespoon almond oil

½ small onion, diced

½ cup diced celery

¾ cup red quinoa

1¾ cups vegetable broth

1 teaspoon kosher salt

1 cup chopped parsley

12 ounces cooked chicken breast, chopped

1 cup sliced almonds, toasted

4 teaspoons fresh lemon juice

½ teaspoon mustard

½ small head green leaf lettuce

½ small head red leaf lettuce

1. Heat 1 tablespoon of the almond oil over medium heat. Add the onion and celery and sweat until soft. Add the quinoa, 1½ cups of the broth, and ½ teaspoon of the salt. Bring to a boil, cover, and simmer until quinoa is soft and the liquid absorbed, about 15 minutes. Allow the quinoa to cool.

2. Stir the parsley, chicken, and ½ cup of the almonds into the quinoa.

3. Combine the lemon juice, mustard, the remaining ¼ cup broth, and the remaining ½ teaspoon salt. Whisk in the remaining ¼ cup almond oil. Toss quinoa salad with half of the dressing. Toss the lettuces with the remaining dressing.

4. Serve the quinoa on a bed of lettuce leaves and top with the reserved ½ cup almonds.

Nutritional Information Per Serving: Calories 354, Protein 19 g, Carbohydrates 22 g, Fiber 4 g, Total Fat 22 g, Saturated Fat 2 g, Sodium 287 mg

Tomato, Chicken, and Feta Cheese with Whole Wheat Fettuccine

This recipe also works well with cooked chicken reserved from making chicken broth. Just add the chicken at the last minute when you toss in the cooked pasta. You can easily double the recipe to serve 4.

1. Bring 2 quarts of water to a boil and add ½ teaspoon of the salt. Cook the fettuccine until al dente, about 10 minutes. Use a slotted spoon to remove the pasta from the water and set aside. Reserve the cooking water.

2. Season the chicken with the remaining ¼ teaspoon salt and the pepper.

3. Heat the olive oil in a sauté pan over medium high heat. When the pan is very hot, add the chicken and brown on both sides. Set the chicken aside and cut into strips. Add the onion to the pan and cook until soft. Add the vinegar and deglaze the pan. Add the tomatoes.

4. Once the tomatoes start to release their water and soften, add the basil and parsley. Return the chicken and pasta to the pan. Add the cheese and toss to coat. Add enough of the reserved pasta cooking water to help form a thin sauce. Finish with a squeeze of fresh lemon juice just before serving.

Nutritional Information Per Serving: Calories 345, Protein 21 g, Carbohydrates 42 g, Fiber 6 g, Total Fat 12 g, Saturated Fat 4 g, Sodium 579 mg

MAKES 2 SERVINGS

¾ teaspoon kosher salt

3 ounces whole wheat fettuccine

¼ teaspoon freshly ground black pepper

2 teaspoons olive oil

2 ounces boneless, skinless chicken breast, pounded to ¼ inch thick

½ small red onion, diced

½ teaspoon white wine vinegar

1 pint grape or cherry tomatoes, halved

1 tablespoon chopped basil

1 tablespoon chopped parsley

2 ounces feta, crumbled

Squeeze of fresh lemon juice

Daikon Spaghetti with Chicken and Tahini Soy Dressing

The Asian daikon radish is a very large, long root vegetable that has a milder flavor than other radishes. Because they are so long you can use a julienne peeler or a mandoline to slice long, thin, strands of "spaghetti".

1. Heat peanut oil in a large sauté pan over medium high heat. Add the garlic and cook just until soft. Add the kale, ¼ teaspoon of the salt, the pepper, and vegetable stock. Cover and steam for 2 minutes.

2. Add the daikon radish and more stock, if necessary, and continue to steam until the vegetables are soft but not mushy.

3. Meanwhile, combine the chicken, dressing, chili sauce, agave syrup, and the remaining ¼ teaspoon salt in a medium saucepan and bring to a simmer.

4. When the vegetables are soft, add the lime juice and cilantro and toss. Top the vegetables with the chicken mixture and peanuts.

Technique Note We use the term "sweat" when we are sautéing with very little oil since the oil is often absorbed before the ingredients have softened. The moisture in the vegetables and any stock, wine, juice, or water added during the cooking process allow the vegetables to continue to soften without burning. If a flavorful liquid is added in small amounts during the process, it reduces and intensifies in flavor.

Nutritional Information Per Serving: Calories 408, Protein 27 g, Carbohydrates 19 g, Fiber 2.5 g, Total Fat 28 g, Saturated Fat 3.5 g, Sodium 688 mg

MAKES 2 SERVINGS

1 teaspoon peanut oil

1 garlic clove, minced

2 cups stems removed and roughly chopped kale leaves

½ teaspoon kosher salt

¼ teaspoon freshly ground black pepper

¼ cup vegetable broth (wild mushroom broth is excellent), plus more as needed

1 daikon radish, julienned lengthwise into "spaghetti" (about 4 cups)

2 cups shredded cooked chicken (5 ounces)

¼ cup Tahini Soy Dressing (page 32)

½ teaspoon hot chili sauce

½ teaspoon agave syrup

2 tablespoons fresh lime juice

¼ cup chopped cilantro

2 tablespoons chopped peanuts

Tomato, Chicken, and Feta Cheese with Whole Wheat Fettuccine

Chicken Paillards with Almond and Orange Dressing

The flavor of almonds in this dish is from the almond butter, which is made like peanut butter, and from almond oil, which is removed from the almonds by pressing. The almond butter and oil add a richness to this dish that would pair well with a fruit-forward Sauvignon Blanc or an unoaked Chardonnay.

1. Trim the chicken breast of excess fat. Pull away the tender from the underside of each breast and reserve for another use. Make a cut through the thickest part of breast to butterfly it.

2. Open each breast between sheets of parchment or plastic wrap and pound it to an even ¼-inch thickness to make a paillard. Season chicken with ¼ teaspoon of the salt and ¼ teaspoon of the pepper.

3. Whisk the almond oil into the orange juice. Stir in 1 teaspoon of the orange zest. Place the paillards in the marinade and marinate the chicken for at least 30 minutes. Remove chicken from the marinade and pat dry.

4. Bring the chicken broth to a simmer. Mix together the remaining orange zest, 1 teaspoon of the thyme, and the remaining salt and pepper. Add the broth and almond butter and mix until well blended and about the consistency of cream. Add a little more or less broth as needed to adjust consistency. Set aside and keep warm.

5. Heat the canola oil in a heavy skillet. When the oil is very hot, cook each breast for 2 to 3 minutes on the first side and 1 to 2 minutes on the second side. Remove from pan and set aside and keep warm.

6. Deglaze the pan with the marinade. Add the chicken and the almond-orange sauce to the pan and toss to coat with sauce. Serve garnished with the remaining thyme.

Nutritional Information Per Serving: Calories 246, Protein 25 g, Carbohydrates 4 g, Total Fat 14 g, Saturated Fat 1.5 g, Sodium 253 mg

MAKES 4 SERVINGS

4 boneless, skinless chicken breasts (about 1 pound)

½ teaspoon kosher salt

½ teaspoon freshly ground black pepper

1 tablespoon almond oil

¼ cup fresh orange juice

2 teaspoons orange zest (about 2 oranges)

¼ cup low-sodium chicken broth, plus more as needed

2 teaspoons minced thyme

3 tablespoons almond butter

1 teaspoon canola oil

Sausage and Barley–Stuffed Peppers, served with Barley Buttermilk Flatbread (page 183)

Sausage and Barley–Stuffed Peppers

After testing the original version, we decided to add spinach and mushrooms to the filling. It made these peppers go from great to fabulous and added a boost to the nutritional profile too.

MAKES 8 SERVINGS

1. Preheat the oven to 400°F.

2. Bring the broth and water to a boil. Add the barley, cover, and reduce the heat to a simmer. Cook the barley until soft but not mushy, about 55 minutes. Set aside and keep warm.

3. Heat the olive oil in a sauté pan over medium high heat. Add the sausage and brown. When the sausage is partially cooked, add the onion, garlic, Italian seasoning, and black pepper. Cook until the onion is soft and sausage is fully cooked, about 2 minutes. Remove from skillet and set aside and keep warm.

4. Add the mushrooms to the pan and sweat until they release most of their liquid. Add the spinach to the pan and cook just until wilted but still bright green. Add the mushroom mixture to the sausage mixture. Add the marinara sauce, barley, and half of the cheese.

5. Stuff each pepper half with 1 cup of the filling. Cover the stuffing of each pepper with a square of foil coated in cooking spray. Place the pepper foil side down in a baking pan. Bake until the juices are bubbling, about 30 minutes.

6. Turn peppers over and remove foil. Sprinkle remaining cheese on top and serve.

Nutritional Information Per Serving: Calories 286, Protein 18 g, Carbohydrates 31 g, Fiber 6.5 g, Total Fat 11 g, Saturated Fat 1.5 g, Sodium 585 mg

2 cups low-sodium chicken broth

1 cup water

1 cup pearled barley

2 teaspoons olive oil

1 pound sweet Italian-style turkey sausage, casings removed

½ medium yellow onion, diced

2 garlic cloves, minced

2 teaspoons Italian seasoning

½ teaspoon freshly ground black pepper

One 8-ounce package sliced mushrooms

5-ounce package spinach leaves, roughly chopped

2 cups marinara sauce (if using jarred, choose low-sodium)

2 ounces Parmesan, grated

4 red bell peppers, cut in half and blanched

Turkey and Sweet Potato Shepherd's Pie

The familiar flavors of the Thanksgiving holiday come together in this shepherd's pie. Individual casseroles freeze well and reheat easily for some quick comfort food all year round. This goes well with a green salad and steamed vegetables on the side.

MAKES 6 SERVINGS

2 medium or 1 large sweet potato (yam), peeled and cut into large chunks

1 tablespoon plus 2 teaspoons canola oil

¾ teaspoon kosher salt

1 teaspoon dried rosemary

1 teaspoon dried sage

1 tablespoon pure maple syrup

One 16-ounce can chickpeas, rinsed, or 2 cups freshly cooked chickpeas

2½ cups plus 2 tablespoons low-sodium chicken broth

1 pound ground turkey (94% lean)

¼ teaspoon freshly ground black pepper

1 tablespoon Bell's Poultry Seasoning

1 yellow onion, diced

2 parsnips, diced

1 stalk celery, diced

8 ounces cremini mushrooms, sliced

½ cup white wine

2 tablespoons all-purpose flour

¼ cup dried cranberries, minced

1 tablespoon unsalted butter

1 tablespoon minced fresh sage leaves

2 tablespoons chopped pecans

1. Preheat the oven to 400°F.

2. Toss the sweet potato chunks with 2 teaspoons of the canola oil, ¼ teaspoon of the salt, the rosemary, and dried sage. Spread the sweet potato chunks onto a baking sheet and roast until very soft and lightly browned, about 45 minutes. Mash the cooked sweet potatoes with the maple syrup. Set aside and keep warm.

3. Purée the chickpeas and ½ cup of the chicken broth in a blender or food processor. Mix with the sweet potatoes and set aside.

4. Heat the remaining 1 tablespoon canola oil in a sauté pan over medium heat heat. Add the ground turkey and brown. Season with the remaining ½ teaspoon salt, the pepper, and 2 teaspoons poultry seasoning. Add the onion, parsnips, and celery once the turkey is no longer pink.

5. Cover and sweat the vegetables until the browned bits of turkey on the bottom of the pan loosen up. Remove the turkey mixture from pan. Set aside and keep warm.

6. Add the mushrooms to the pan and gradually add ¼ cup of the white wine to help the mushrooms sweat until soft. Allow the wine and mushroom liquid to almost evaporate. Sprinkle the mushrooms with flour and the remaining 1 teaspoon poultry seasoning. Allow the flour and mushrooms to cook slightly but do not allow to burn.

7. Add the turkey mixture back to the pan and mix with the mushrooms to combine. Add 2 cups of the chicken broth and bring to a gentle boil.

8. Meanwhile, simmer the cranberries in the remaining ¼ cup white wine until soft and the volume of the wine is reduced by half. Add the cranberry mixture to the turkey mixture.

9. Put the turkey mixture in a small casserole or pie plate and spread the top with the mashed sweet potato mixture.

10. Melt the butter and sauté the fresh sage leaves briefly to release their flavor. Whisk in the remaining 2 tablespoons chicken broth and allow to reduce slightly. Pour over the casserole and top with the pecans.

11. Bake until mixture is hot and bubbly, about 15 minutes, and serve.

Nutritional Information Per Serving: Calories 424, Protein 23 g, Carbohydrates 53 g, Fiber 8.5 g, Total Fat 13 g, Saturated Fat 3 g, Sodium 387 mg

Turkey Meatloaf

The portobello mushrooms add umami flavor to mimic the beef flavors of traditional meatloaf in this healthier version that is lower in saturated fat. No gravy is needed since this meatloaf is very moist.

1. Preheat oven to 325°F.

2. Heat the olive oil in sauté pan over medium high heat. Add the onion and cook until it begins to soften. Add the mushrooms and cook until soft but not browned. Add the Worcestershire sauce, salt, pepper, thyme, rosemary, and tomato paste and stir to mix.

3. Mix the broth with the oats to moisten. Stir in the egg. Combine the onion mixture, oats mixture, and ground turkey and mix well. Form the mixture into a loaf on an ungreased baking sheet. Bake for 45 minutes, then spread the ketchup on top of the meatloaf. Bake 45 minutes more, or until cooked to an internal temperature of 165°F.

Nutritional Information Per Serving: Calories 314, Protein 32 g, Carbohydrates 14 g, Fiber 1.5 g, Total Fat 14.5 g, Saturated Fat 3.5 g, Sodium 589 mg

MAKES 4 SERVINGS

1 tablespoon olive oil

½ medium yellow onion, diced

4 ounces baby portobello mushrooms, finely diced

2 tablespoons Worcestershire sauce

½ teaspoon kosher salt

½ teaspoon freshly ground black pepper

¼ teaspoon dried thyme

½ teaspoon dried rosemary

1 teaspoon tomato paste

⅓ cup reduced-sodium canned chicken broth

½ cup old-fashioned oats, chopped to the size of bread crumbs

1 egg

One 20.8-ounce package ground turkey

¼ cup ketchup

Sweet-'n'-Sour Pork-'n'-Beans

Professor John Canner, who teaches menu development at the Hyde Park campus of The Culinary Institute of America, requested a recipe that uses a slow cooker. Pork and beans seemed like an obvious choice, so here is a vegetable-rich version with a nice balance of sweet and sour flavors. You can also use beans that have been cooked in advance and frozen. Just add the frozen beans to the slow cooker with the vegetables.

1. Soak the beans in water for several hours or overnight until they start to absorb some of the soaking water or refer to page 136 for the quick soak method. Drain the soaking water. Combine the beans and beef broth and simmer until the beans are soft, 1 to 1½ hours. Do not allow to boil or the skins on the beans will break.

2. Mix the tomato purée, cider vinegar, coffee, Worcestershire sauce, soy sauce, agave syrup, maple flavoring, garlic, mustard, oregano, ¾ teaspoon of the black pepper, and the cayenne in a sauce pan. Simmer while you prepare the pork.

3. Cut the pork into 3 to 4 large pieces and season with the salt and the remaining ¼ teaspoon black pepper. Heat the canola oil in a heavy skillet over medium high heat. Sear the pork until well browned. Remove from the skillet and set aside.

4. Add the onion to the pan and cook until soft and golden brown. Place the sauce, onion, pork, and shredded apple in a slow cooker. Cover and cook on medium high until the pork shreds with a fork, about 3 hours. Add in the red and yellow peppers, the cabbage, and beans. Allow to simmer until the vegetables are soft.

Nutritional Information Per Serving: Calories 352, Protein 22 g, Carbohydrates 47 g, Fiber 9 g, Total Fat 10 g, Saturated Fat 3 g, Sodium 509 mg

MAKES 8 SERVINGS

1 cup dried baby borlotta beans

2 cups beef broth

One 28-ounce can tomato purée

⅔ cup apple cider vinegar

⅓ cup brewed coffee

3 tablespoons Worcestershire sauce

2 tablespoons reduced-sodium soy sauce

½ cup agave syrup

1½ teaspoons maple-flavoring extract

3 large garlic cloves, minced

2½ teaspoons dry mustard

1½ teaspoons dried oregano

1 teaspoon freshly ground black pepper

½ teaspoon cayenne

1½ pounds boneless pork shoulder (picnic roast)

½ teaspoon kosher salt

1 tablespoon canola oil

1 medium onion, chopped

1 Granny Smith apple, shredded

1 red bell pepper, chopped (about 1 cup)

1 yellow bell pepper, chopped (about 1 cup)

2 cups chopped red cabbage

Caraway-Herb Roasted Pork Tenderloin

This pork is just as good as leftovers as it is warm from the oven. To make a complete meal, try it with the Roasted Carrots and Celeriac with Fennel Seeds *(page 170)*, a garnish of Peperonata *(page 149)* and the Lentil and Parsley Salad with Mustard-Sherry Vinaigrette *(page 175)*. A light to medium-bodied red wine such as a Beaujolais or Pinot Noir would be nice with the earthy flavors in this dish. A barrel-fermented Chardonnay would also work well with this meal.

MAKES 4 SERVINGS

1 tablespoon balsamic vinegar
1 tablespoon olive oil
1 teaspoon dried thyme
1 teaspoon dried oregano
1 tablespoon caraway seeds
4 shallots, finely minced
2 large garlic cloves, minced
1 teaspoon coarse sea salt
1 pound pork tenderloin

1. Combine the vinegar, olive oil, thyme, oregano, caraway seeds, shallots, garlic, and salt. Spread the mixture on the pork tenderloin. Wrap the tenderloin tightly in plastic wrap and chill for at least 2 hours and up to overnight in the refrigerator.

2. Preheat the oven to 350°F. Remove the pork from the plastic wrap.

3. Roast the pork until it registers 145°F on a meat thermometer, about 45 minutes. After 30 minutes, raise the oven temperature to 450°F for the remaining cooking time.

4. Remove from oven and allow the tenderloin to rest for 10 minutes covered with a foil tent. Slice thinly and serve.

Nutritional Information Per Serving: Calories 181, Protein 25 g, Carbohydrates 6 g, Fiber 0.5 g, Total Fat 6 g, Saturated Fat 1.5 g, Sodium 541 mg

OPPOSITE: Caraway-Herb Roasted Pork Tenderloin, served with Peperonata (page 149), Lentil and Parsley Salad with Mustard-Sherry Vinaigrette (page 175), and Roasted Carrots and Celeriac with Fennel Seeds (page 170)

London Broil with Brykill Farm Beef Rub

Brykill Farm is a family-owned natural beef ranch where the cattle graze on 450 acres of lush, organically maintained pastures in Gardiner, New York. Owner Susan Eckhardt created this beef rub, which is just as good on a roast as it is on a London broil or strip steak.

1. For the rub, mix all of the ingredients together and store in an airtight container. This mixture can be stored for up to 6 months.

2. Preheat the oven to 350°F.

3. Rub about 2 tablespoons of the spice mix onto the meat and chill for at least 1 hour or up to overnight.

4. Sear the meat on the grill or in a heavy pan on both sides, about 3 minutes per side. Finish the meat in the oven, cooking until the internal temperature registers 140 to 145° F on a meat thermometer, about 15 minutes. Allow the meat to rest for 10 minutes before slicing.

Nutritional Information Per Serving: Calories 172, Protein 22 g, Carbohydrates 0 g, Fiber 0 g, Total Fat 8 g, Saturated Fat 2.5 g, Sodium 224 mg

Nutritional Information Per Tablespoon of Dry Rub: Calories 7, Protein 0 g, Carbohydrates 1 g, Fiber 0 g, Total Fat 0 g, Saturated Fat 0 g, Sodium 619 mg

MAKES 8 SERVINGS

DRY RUB

2 tablespoons dried oregano

1 tablespoon dried thyme

1 tablespoon dried rosemary

2 teaspoons garlic powder

1 teaspoon ground fennel seed

1 teaspoon celery seed

1 teaspoon dried lemon peel

2 tablespoons coarse sea salt

2 tablespoons freshly ground black pepper

2 pounds boneless chuck, London broil

London Broil with Brykill Farm Beef Rub, served
with Broccoli Rabe with Roasted Red Peppers
and Italian "Sausage" Vinaigrette (page 142) and
Smashed Calypso Beans and Butter (page 177)

Beef Braised in Beer and Onions

Beer, onions, beef…need I say any more? Serve it with the Caraway Cauliflower Mash *(page 145)* for a hearty, stick-to-your-ribs meal that is not loaded with fat or salt, but has the succulence of a stew.

1. Preheat the oven to 350°F.

2. Season the meat with the salt and pepper and dredge in the flour. Heat the canola oil in a heavy Dutch oven over medium high heat. Sear both sides of the meat and set aside.

3. Reduce heat to medium, and add the sliced onions to the Dutch oven and brown slowly, 15 to 20 minutes. Add the minced garlic and continue to cook until the garlic is soft. Return the meat to the pan and add the beef broth, beer, and tomatoes.

4. Cover and braise in the oven, about 1½ hours.

5. Tie the whole garlic clove, the chopped onion, carrot, celery, parsnip, bay leaf, parsley, thyme, and peppercorns in cheesecloth to make a sachet and add to the stew.

6. Allow the stew to braise until the meat is fork tender, about 30 minutes more. Cool the stew and chill overnight. Skim the solid fat off the top of the stew before rewarming to serve. (If desired, you can thicken the stew with a paste of 1 teaspoon arrowroot and 1 tablespoon water.)

Note A heavy pan is best for searing the beef. It conducts heat evenly so the food browns with less risk of burning. Start with a very hot pan and make sure the surface of the meat is dry so it does not steam in its own moisture. The meat should sizzle when it hits the pan. Do not turn it until the bottom is very well browned, which will take several minutes. You can reduce the heat slightly once the browning has started to avoid burning. This process creates deep, rich flavors in the finished dish.

Nutritional Information Per Serving: Calories 347, Protein 25 g, Carbohydrates 15 g, Fiber 2 g, Total Fat 18.5 g, Saturated Fat 6 g, Sodium 201 mg

OPPOSITE: Beef Braised in Beer and Onions, served with Roasted Radishes (page 156) and Caraway Cauliflower Mash (page 145)

RIGHT: Sear the meat until nicely browned in a very hot Dutch oven to develop flavor.

MAKES 8 SERVINGS

2 pounds boneless chuck pot roast

¾ teaspoon kosher salt

½ teaspoon freshly ground black pepper

1 tablespoon all-purpose flour

2 tablespoons canola oil

4 medium onions, sliced

5 garlic cloves, 4 minced and 1 whole

1 quart low-sodium beef broth

1 pint dark beer

One 14.5-ounce can low-sodium diced tomatoes

½ small onion, chopped

1 small carrot, chopped

1 stalk celery, chopped

1 small parsnip, chopped

1 bay leaf

1 parsley sprig

1 thyme sprig

3 black peppercorns

Arrowroot paste, *(optional)*

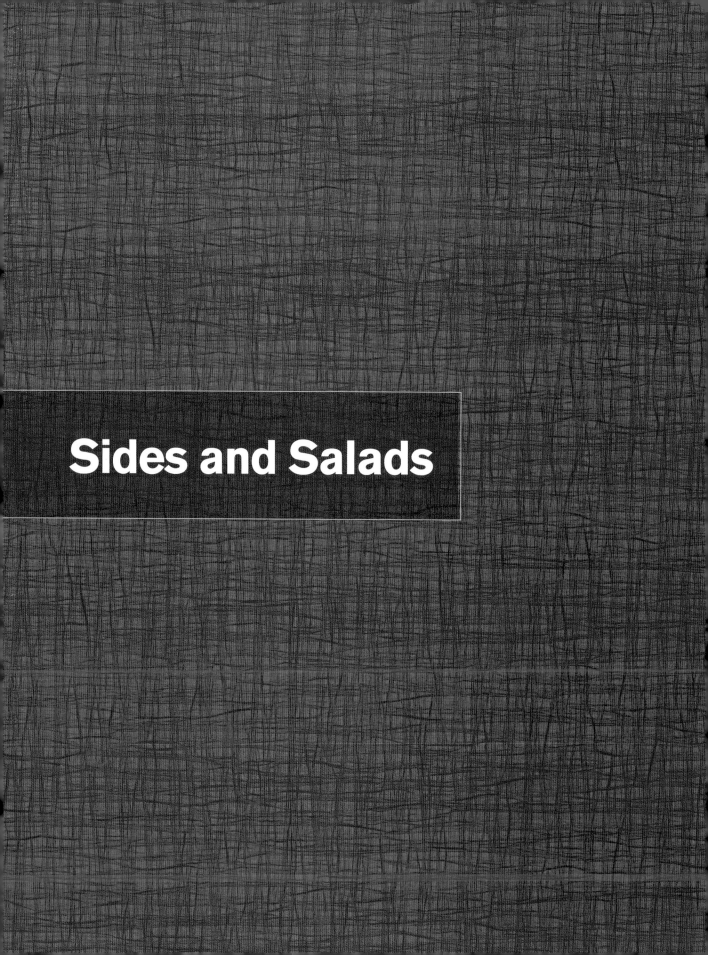

Sides and Salads

Side dishes can add low-calorie flavor and textures to a meal along with fiber and antioxidants. Or they can be the downfall of an otherwise healthy dining experience. Starchy side dishes like potatoes, rice, and pasta are often served in large portions that end up pushing the total carbohydrate and calorie count for a meal over the edge. Your blood glucose can suffer as a result. There are several strategies for tackling this problem. First, select lots of vegetables and minimally processed, high-fiber starches as your sides. Whole grains such as quinoa, pearled barley, legumes, and steel-cut oats are diabetes-friendly side dishes because they are rich in fiber and tend to result in a more gradual rise in blood glucose levels. Consider mixing these starches with your old favorites. For instance, mashed white beans can be mixed with mashed potatoes and you can make a white rice and quinoa pilaf to help your palate adjust to the different taste and textures of whole grains and legumes.

Clearly, if portions of the starchy side dishes are to remain modest you need to fill your plate with low-carbohydrate vegetables that you enjoy to keep the meal filling. Following is a list of 15 fabulous vegetables that are low in carbohydrates. They are on the *must try and keep on hand* list not only because they are low in carbohydrates, but because of their flexibility in recipes (mushrooms, celery, cucumbers), ability to hold well (cabbage, cauliflower, radishes, fennel), or they are packed with phytonutrients and antioxidants (arugula, broccoli rabe, bell peppers, kale) and they taste great.

Table 5.1 The Fabulous Flavorful Fifteen Vegetables

Vegetable	Portion Size	Carbohydrate Amount
Arugula	½ cup	½ g
Bell pepper, green	½ cup, sliced	2 g
Bell pepper, red	½ cup, sliced	3 g
Bell pepper, yellow	½ cup, sliced	3 g
Broccoli rabe	½ cup cooked	3 g
Cucumber	½ cup, sliced	1.5 g
Cauliflower	½ cup cooked	2.5 g
Cabbage, green or savoy	½ cup cooked ½ cup raw, shredded	4 g 2 g
Celery	2 medium stalks	2.5 g
Fennel bulb	½ cup raw, sliced	3 g
Kale	½ cup cooked	4 g
Mushrooms	½ cup cooked	2 g
Radishes	½ cup	2g
Spinach	½ cup cooked	3.5 g
Sugar snap peas	½ cup raw	2 g

Variety in Vegetables

The type of vegetables you use and how you prepare them will impact the final flavor and texture. There is a huge difference between broccoli fresh from the farmer's market and frozen chopped broccoli. Frozen is not necessarily inferior to the fresh, they are just different. So try vegetables in a variety of forms and preparations before you decide you don't like it. A basic vinaigrette recipe can be used to keep the vegetables interesting and appealing. Vinaigrettes are generally thought of as a simple salad dressing, but they can also be used as marinades, sauces, or glazes on other items as well.

Vinaigrette Basic Technique

1. Combine the vinegar with the seasoning ingredients first, reserving the oil. This evenly disperses all of the ingredients which will make it easier to emulsify the vinaigrette when the oil is added.

2. Add the oil gradually, whisking constantly, until the mixture is thick and emulsified. Check the final seasoning before serving.

General Guidelines for Preparing Vegetables

Each vegetable cooking technique produces specific results that affect the flavor, texture, and nutritive value of each vegetable in different ways. The correct level of doneness in a vegetable can vary depending on cooking method and type of vegetable. For example, stir-frying generally results in a crisp texture, while braising results in very tender vegetables. Some vegetables, such as broccoli and green beans, are not considered properly cooked unless they are very tender. Other vegetables, such as sugar snap peas, should always retain some bite.

Steamed Vegetables

Steamed vegetables are cooked in a vapor bath of steam. Steaming shares many similarities with boiling, though steamed foods can be more flavorful, have better texture, and are said to have higher nutritional value than boiled vegetables because fewer nutrients are lost in the cooking liquid. Tiered steamers or steamer pots work best for large amounts of vegetables.

Steaming Vegetables Basic Technique

1. Bring the liquid to a full boil in the bottom of a covered steamer. Arrange vegetables in a single layer to allow the steam to come in contact with all sides of the vegetables.

2. Seasonings should be added to the vegetables or the liquid prior to beginning steaming. Bring the liquid to a boil, and cover the pot. Continue to cook the vegetables to desired doneness.

Pan-Steamed Vegetables

Pan-steaming is an excellent (and quick) technique for small batches or individual servings. Pan steamed vegetables are prepared in a covered pot with a small amount of liquid. This technique can be done quickly, and flavorful liquids can be used during cooking to impart flavor or become a sort of "sauce" after steaming.

Pan-Steaming Vegetables Basic Technique

1. Pour or ladle enough cooking liquid into the pan to properly cook the vegetables. Dense vegetables will need more liquid than tender vegetables.

2. Check the vegetables periodically during cooking to check their doneness and maintain the proper level of heat.

3. Cook the vegetables to their desired doneness (pan-steaming can be used to blanch, parcook, or fully cook vegetables). Drain the vegetables from the cooking liquid or reduce and season the liquid to make a sauce/glaze for the finished vegetables.

Boiled Vegetables

Boiling is a basic technique often used to cook starchy root vegetables. Keep in mind that the longer a vegetable is in the water the more of the vitamin C and B complex vitamins that will leach into the water. Boiled vegetables can be served chilled, added to another dish to finish cooking, used to make a purée, or simply eaten alone. Use a pot that will comfortably hold the vegetables being boiled. Have a strainer or colander on hand for straining the finished vegetables.

Boiling Vegetables Basic Technique

1. Season the cooking liquid and bring it to the correct temperature before adding the vegetables. Salting the cooking water will result in an unpredictable amount of sodium being added to the vegetable. If you have been encouraged to limit your salt or sodium intake experiment cooking the vegetables with less salt or none at all. Though the amount of liquid can vary depending on the vegetable, there should usually be enough water to hold the vegetables comfortably without overcrowding them.

2. Bring the water to a rolling boil (for starchy root vegetables, start with cool water and bring it to a gentle boil — this will promote even cooking). Add the vegetables to the pot, and if necessary, bring it back to a rapid simmer. Cook the vegetables to the appropriate doneness.

3. Drain the vegetables. They are now ready to be finished and served.

Grilled and Broiled Vegetables

Cooking vegetables over an intense, direct heat, such as that from a grill or broiler, gives them a rich, bold flavor. Scour the rods of your grill or broiler before and after grilling to remove any buildup or charred food. Remember that some vegetables (such as thick-cut vegetables or those high in starch) can retain heat after they are removed from the grill or broiler.

Grilling or Broiling Vegetables Basic Technique

1. Place the prepared vegetables directly on the grill or broiler rods. If using a glaze or marinade, gently brush a light coat on the vegetables during cooking. Salt, pepper, and other dry seasonings should be added when the vegetables are finished cooking and off the grill.

2. Grill or broil the vegetables, turning as necessary, until they have reached the desired doneness. To create crosshatch marks, give the vegetables a 90-degree turn after the grill rods have made an imprint, and allow the rods to imprint again.

Roasted and Baked Vegetables

Roasting and baking are versatile cooking techniques. Thick-skinned vegetables, for example, can be roasted or baked to soften their skin and flesh. Mirepoix or aromatic vegetables can be roasted or baked to add color and intensify their flavor. Tomatoes or peppers can be roasted or baked to give them a drier texture. Use roasting pans or baking sheets that are large enough to accommodate the vegetables without overcrowding.

Roasting or Baking Vegetables Basic Technique

1. Place the prepared vegetables into a roasting pan or baking sheet. Vegetables can be seasoned prior to cooking and, in some circumstances, liquid can be added to help steam dense vegetables and prevent scorching.

2. Roast the vegetables until tender and cooked through. While length of time and temperature will be determined largely by the type of vegetable, its cut, and its thickness, a general rule is that the longer the cooking time, the lower the oven temperature should be.

Sautéed and Stir-Fried Vegetables

Sautéing and stir-frying are simple techniques where vegetables are cooked in a small amount of fat. Select vegetable oils instead of solid fats to limit the amount of artery-clogging saturated fats you are adding to your meal. Use the oil sparingly since even the heart-healthy oils are high in calories. These techniques can be used to cook many vegetables, as well as finishing them just prior to serving; some vegetables will not cook completely when sautéed unless par-cooked with another method first. Be sure to use a pan large enough to hold the vegetables without overcrowding; if too much is in the pan, the temperature will drop quickly. If the pan itself is too large, it may lead to scorching.

Sautéing and Stir-Frying Vegetables Basic Technique

1. Add the prepared vegetables to the fat and (if using) the sweated aromatics in the pan. Vegetables require less intense heat than meat, poultry, and fish, and the fat should be hot but not hazy or smoking.

2. Sauté the vegetables until they reach the correct level of doneness. If more than one type of vegetable is being sautéed, the vegetables should be added in sequence, starting with the vegetable requiring the most time to cook, so that they are finished at the same time.

Stewed and Braised Vegetables

Stewed and braised vegetables cook in their own juices. Vegetables can be cut into small pieces and stewed, while larger or whole pieces are generally braised. The liquid can be reduced or thickened to give it more body, or the juices can merely act as a simple glaze or sauce on the finished vegetables. Use a deep, wide cooking vessel with a lid to stew or braise.

Stewing and Braising Vegetables Basic Technique

1. Cook the aromatic vegetables until tender to develop flavor to the dish.

2. Add the prepared vegetables in sequence (from firmest to most tender) and braise or stew until the vegetables are fully cooked, tender, and flavorful.

3. When the vegetables are cooked, the liquid can be reduced into a sauce, or some of the vegetable can be puréed with the liquid to create a sauce.

Whole Grains and Legumes

Whole grains have not been milled; the grain is fully intact and maintains the full nutritional content of the bran, germ, and hull. Some varieties of whole grains include: wheat berries, brown rice, rye berries, amaranth, spelt, quinoa, and pearled barley. The less processed the grain, the slower your blood glucose will rise after eating it. For example, steel-cut oats will raise your blood glucose less than the same amount of quick-cooking oats and wheat berries may be better tolerated than whole wheat couscous, which is more processed. The recipes here include mostly grains and starches that have a low glycemic impact so they are less likely to result in a rapid rise in your blood glucose.

Grains and legumes are dried foods that must be rehydrated before they can be eaten. They should be carefully sorted before cooking to remove stones or other impurities, and rinsed before cooking begins. Water and broth are most commonly used for the cooking liquid, and seasonings can be added before, during, or after cooking depending on the desired result. Generally, grains and legumes are cooked in more liquid than they can actually absorb; this keeps the grains fluffy and separated after cooking. Use a pot large enough to allow for the expansion of the grains as they cook.

Dried beans require a little advance planning to include them in a meal. If you are not happy with the dried beans available at the grocery store shop online for heirloom varieties of beans (see page 16). They are more expensive but the flavor, texture, and appearance are superior to mass-produced beans. Like vegetables, the quality, flavor, and texture of beans can vary greatly. Canned beans are usually higher in sodium than dried beans and may have a mushier texture. The flavor and texture of a canned bean can even vary from one brand to another so experiment with different brands.

Soaking Legumes

Some legumes benefit from soaking prior to cooking. Soaking softens their skins, allowing for more even and rapid cooking. Soaking time will vary based on the type of legume. Occasionally dried beans don't soften fully from the soaking and cooking; this may happen if the beans are really old. There are two commonly used soaking methods:

The long soak method. Place sorted and rinsed legumes in a large bowl and add enough cool water to cover them by about 2 inches. Let them soak, refrigerated, for the required time.

The short soak method. Place the sorted and rinsed legumes in a pot and add enough water to cover by about 2 inches. Bring the water to a simmer, then remove the pot from the heat and cover. Let the legumes steep for 1 hour.

Approximate Soaking and Cooking Times for Selected Dried Legumes

Type	Soaking Time	Cooking Time
Adzuki beans	4 hours	1 hour
Black beans	4 hours	1½ hours
Black-eyed peas*	—	1 hour
Chickpeas	4 hours	2 to 2½ hours
Fava beans	12 hours	3 hours
Great Northern beans	4 hours	1 hour
Kidney beans (red or white)	4 hours	1 hour
Heirloom beans	4 hours	30 to 45 minutes
Lentils*	—	30 to 40 minutes
Lima beans	4 hours	1 to 1½ hours
Mung beans	4 hours	1 hour
Navy beans	4 hours	2 hours
Peas, split*	—	30 minutes
Peas, whole	4 hours	40 minutes
Pigeon peas*	—	30 minutes
Pink beans	4 hours	1 hour
Pinto beans	4 hours	1 to 1½ hours
Soybeans	12 hours	3 to 3½ hours

*Soaking is not necessary

Simmering Grains and Legumes Basic Technique

1. Combine the grains or legumes with the cooking liquid and bring to a full boil. Reduce the heat, cover and simmer the grains or legumes until tender.

2. Check the level of the cooking liquid throughout the cooking time, adding more as needed to keep them fully covered.

3. If the cooking liquid is not entirely absorbed during the cooking process, drain the grains or legumes.

Simmered and Boiled Grains

When grains are milled they produce cereals and meals. The results range from coarse, such as cracked wheat, to fine, such as cornmeal. The finer the milling, the quicker the grain is digested and raises blood glucose. Water, broth, or milk is the most common cooking liquid, and most grains are cooked in the amount of liquid they can absorb during cooking. Use a pot with a heavy bottom to prevent scorching and remember to budget in the carbohydrate present in the cooking liquid if you are using milk.

Simmering and Boiling Grains Basic Technique

1. Bring the liquid to a full boil and add the grains in a thin stream, stirring constantly. Some grains should be combined with the liquid and then brought to a boil; see specific recipes for more instruction.

2. Reduce the heat, and simmer, stirring occasionally, until the grain has thickened and is fully cooked. Some meals or cereals become stiff and pull away from the pot, while others remain fluid.

Pilaf

In a pilaf, the grain, usually rice, is first heated in a pot, and then combined with hot liquid. The pot is covered and the grain is cooked, either over direct heat or in the oven. Pilafs can be simple—just grain—or it can be a composed dish with additional ingredients. Adding extra diced vegetables at the end of cooking adds flavor, fiber, and increases the portion size without adding a lot of extra carbohydrates. Use a large heavy pot with a lid, which allows the grains to steam.

Cooking Pilaf Basic Technique

1. Sweat any aromatics, if using, until softened. Add the grains and sauté, stirring frequently, until parched.

2. Heat the cooking liquid, and add it to the grains. Bring the mixture to a steady simmer, stirring occasionally.

3. Cover the pot and cook for the required time, either on the stovetop or in the oven, per specific recipe instructions. Remove the pot from the heat and allow the pilaf to rest, covered, about 5 minutes before serving.

Risotto

Risotto is a rich, creamy dish made from grains. Traditionally, it is made with rice, but certain other grains can be substituted and cooked utilizing the same technique. Pearled barley can be used to make risotto and it is less likely to raise blood glucose levels rapidly as it is rich in fiber and has a low glycemic impact. The grain is parched, but the cooking liquid is added and absorbed gradually while the grain is stirred almost constantly. The starch slowly releases during the cooking process, producing the dish's characteristic texture. Many risotto recipes call for butter, cheese, or cream to be added. Avoid these additions, as they add a lot of saturated fat, which should use sparingly by a person with diabetes. Use a wide pan with a heavy bottom to prevent scorching.

Cooking Risotto Basic Technique

1. Sweat any aromatics, if using, until softened. Add the grains and sauté, stirring frequently, until parched.

2. Heat the cooking liquid, and add it to the grain gradually. Start by adding about one-quarter of the cooking liquid and stir constantly over medium heat until the liquid is absorbed.

3. Continue adding the hot liquid, one-quarter at a time and stirring constantly until absorbed, until all the liquid is incorporated, the grains are tender, and the grains have a creamy consistency.

Arugula and Spinach Salad with Raspberry Dressing

The natural sweetness of the raspberries tastes fantastic with the slightly bitter arugula and also pairs beautifully with the spinach. The bright berry flavors are complemented by the red wine and balsamic vinegars in a vinaigrette that is extremely easy to make.

1. For the vinaigrette, combine the vinegars and salt and add the raspberries. Whisk in the olive oil.

2. Add the spinach and arugula to the vinaigrette and toss gently. When the greens are lightly coated, transfer to chilled plates, and finish with a generous grinding of pepper.

Nutritional Information Per Serving: Calories 78, Protein 0.5 g, Carbohydrates 5 g, Fiber 1 g, Total Fat 7 g, Saturated Fat 1 g, Sodium 70 mg

MAKES 6 SERVINGS

1 tablespoon red wine vinegar
1 tablespoon balsamic vinegar
¼ teaspoon kosher salt
1 cup mashed raspberries
3 tablespoons olive oil
3 cups baby spinach leaves
3 cups arugula
Freshly ground black pepper

Broccoli Rabe with Roasted Red Peppers and Italian "Sausage" Vinaigrette

The seasoning blend in Italian sweet sausage is used to make the vinaigrette that dresses the slightly bitter broccoli rabe and sweet, smoky roasted red peppers *(see photo on page 125)*. This side dish pairs wonderfully with the Sausage and Barley–Stuffed Peppers *(page 117)*.

MAKES 8 SERVINGS

1 bunch broccoli rabe, ends trimmed and blanched

1 red bell pepper, skin charred and removed

½ lemon, juiced, plus more as needed

1 tablespoon brown sugar

¼ teaspoon fennel seed, crushed

½ teaspoon Italian seasoning

½ teaspoon dried sage

½ teaspoon kosher salt

¼ teaspoon freshly ground black pepper, plus more as needed

Pinch ground cloves

Pinch cayenne

2 tablespoons olive oil

1. Chop the broccoli rabe into 1- to 2-inch pieces. Remove and discard the stem and seeds from the roasted red pepper. Dice the red pepper.

2. Mix the lemon juice, brown sugar, fennel, Italian seasoning, sage, salt, black pepper, cloves, and cayenne. Whisk in the olive oil.

3. Heat a pan over medium high heat. Add the broccoli rabe, red pepper, and vinaigrette and sauté until hot and broccoli rabe stems are tender.

3. Season with additional black pepper and lemon juice, if desired.

Nutritional Information Per Serving: Calories 58, Protein 2 g, Carbohydrates 4 g, Fiber 1.5 g, Total Fat 4 g, Saturated Fat 0.5 g, Sodium 101 mg

Cucumber Salad with Cider-Dijon Vinaigrette

This salad is very easy to put together quickly if you have last-minute dinner guests coming or are just home from a long day at work. If you prefer less raw-onion flavor, soak the sliced onions in ice water for 10 to 15 minutes before preparing the dish.

Mix together the vinegar, mustard, salt, and pepper. Mix together the cucumbers, onion, and parsley. Drizzle the vinaigrette over the vegetables and toss.

Nutritional Information Per Serving: Calories 25, Protein 2 g, Carbohydrates 5 g, Fiber 2 g, Total Fat 0 g, Saturated Fat 0 g, Sodium 312 mg

MAKES 2 SERVINGS

2 teaspoons cider vinegar

½ teaspoon Dijon mustard

½ teaspoon kosher salt

⅛ teaspoon freshly ground black pepper

1 medium cucumber, peeled, seeded, and thinly sliced

¼ red onion, thinly sliced

4 parsley sprigs, stems removed and leaves minced

Cucumber, Onion, and Parsley Salad with Feta

These ingredients have been paired in the Mediterranean for ages with good reason. Although this salad is simple, each ingredient brings a unique flavor and texture that combine to make a delicious side dish.

1. Mix together the salt, pepper, and lemon juice. Whisk in the olive oil.

2. Combine the cucumber, onion, and parsley. Drizzle the vinaigrette over the vegetables and toss. Sprinkle the feta over the top.

Nutritional Information Per Serving: Calories 127, Protein 3 g, Carbohydrates 7 g, Fiber 2.5 g, Total Fat 10.5 g, Saturated Fat 2 g, Sodium 350 mg

MAKES 2 SERVINGS

½ teaspoon kosher salt

⅛ teaspoon freshly ground black pepper

1 tablespoon fresh lemon juice

4 teaspoons olive oil

1 medium cucumber, peeled, seeded, and thinly sliced

¼ red onion, thinly sliced

4 parsley sprigs, stems removed and leaves minced

2 tablespoons crumbled feta cheese

Caraway Cauliflower Mash

Cauliflower takes the place of some of the potato in this side. Caraway adds an intriguing flavor and Greek yogurt replaces the cream to make a healthy version of mashed potatoes *(see photo on page 126)*. This recipe was created by Melia Kilbourn a student in the Bachelors of Professional Studies program at The Culinary Institute of America.

1. Preheat the oven to 350°F.

2. Coat the cauliflower and potato with the olive oil and ¼ teaspoon of the salt and place on a baking sheet. Roast until soft and lightly browned, about 1 hour.

3. Steep the caraway seeds in the evaporated milk for ten minutes. Strain and discard the seeds.

4. Melt the butter in a medium sauce pot. Add the shallot and leeks and sauté until soft and translucent. Add the caraway-infused milk.

5. Purée the roasted vegetables and the shallot-leek mixture in a blender or food processor until just barely smooth. Stir in the yogurt and season with the remaining salt.

Nutritional Information Per Serving: Calories 117, Protein 5 g, Carbohydrates 16 g, Fiber 3 g, Total Fat 5 g, Saturated Fat 2 g, Sodium 148 mg

MAKES 6 SERVINGS

1 head cauliflower, core removed and cut into 1-inch-thick slices

1 white potato, peeled and quartered

1 tablespoon olive oil

½ teaspoon kosher salt

½ teaspoon caraway seeds

¼ cup evaporated 2% milk

1 tablespoon unsalted butter

½ shallot, minced

⅓ cup thinly sliced leeks, white and light green part

¼ teaspoon kosher salt

¼ cup nonfat Greek yogurt, warmed gently on the stove

Curried Cauliflower "Couscous"

Curry is a classic seasoning used on cauliflower in Indian cuisine and this recipe presents this classic combination in a new way. This mock couscous can be used as a bed for simple roasted vegetables and grilled chicken.

MAKES 4 SERVINGS

1 head of cauliflower, core removed

2 tablespoons olive oil

1 tablespoon curry powder

1 teaspoon ground cumin

¼ teaspoon kosher salt

¼ teaspoon freshly ground black pepper

1. Preheat the oven to 400°F.

2. Break cauliflower into florets, slicing the larger florets in half. Toss the cauliflower with the olive oil, curry powder, and cumin. Place the florets on a greased baking sheet and roast until golden brown, about 30 minutes.

3. Pulse the roasted cauliflower in a food processor until the cauliflower is fluffy and the size of couscous. Return the "couscous" to the baking sheet and heat in the oven, about 10 minutes more. Sprinkle with the salt and pepper and serve.

Nutritional Information Per Serving: Calories 67, Protein 2 g, Carbohydrates 5 g, Fiber 2 g, Total Fat 5 g, Saturated Fat 1 g, Sodium 75 mg

Roast the cauliflower, and then process in a food processor until the mixture is crumbly.

Cabbage, Celery, and Carrot Salad with Sesame Dressing

Savoy cabbage makes for a beautiful side dish because of the different shades of green and white in the leaves and the crinkly texture that is its trademark. Cabbage is a classic ingredient in Asian cuisine and it tastes extraordinary with this sesame dressing.

1. Combine the celery, carrots, cabbage, and cilantro.

2. Mix together the vinegar and soy sauce. Whisk in the sesame oil.

3. Add the peanuts to the vegetables. Drizzle with the dressing and toss.

Nutritional Information Per Serving: Calories 99, Protein 3.5 g, Carbohydrates 8 g, Fiber 3 g, Total Fat 7 g, Saturated Fat 1 g, Sodium 147 mg

MAKES 4 SERVINGS

3 stalks celery, thinly sliced on the bias

2 carrots, peeled and julienned

1 cup shredded savoy cabbage

3 tablespoons chopped cilantro

1 tablespoon rice wine vinegar

½ teaspoon reduced-sodium soy sauce

2 teaspoons pure sesame oil

¼ cup peanuts, chopped

Warm Cabbage Salad

This is filling comfort food that has no hint of "diet" to it. It can be served warm or at room temperature.

1. In a large skillet cook the bacon until the fat renders and the bacon is crisp, 8 to 10 minutes. Remove from the pan, drain, and reserve the cooked bacon. Add the onion and garlic to the same pan and sauté until the onions are translucent, 5 to 8 minutes.

2. Combine the chicken broth, vinegar, wine, sugar, and salt and stir to dissolve the sugar. Add the broth mixture, cabbage, and caraway seeds to the skillet. Cook until the cabbage is limp and tender, about 10 minutes. Remove from the heat and stir in the parsley and reserved bacon. Serve warm or at room temperature.

Nutritional Information Per Serving: Calories 74, Protein 3.5 g, Carbohydrates 11 g, Fiber 4 g, Total Fat 2.5 g, Saturated Fat 1 g, Sodium 158 mg

MAKES 4 SERVINGS

1 slice bacon, diced

⅓ cup diced red onion

1 garlic clove, minced

3 tablespoons low-sodium chicken broth

1½ tablespoons tarragon vinegar

1½ tablespoons dry white wine

2 teaspoons sugar

¼ teaspoon kosher salt

7½ cups shredded savoy cabbage

¼ teaspoon caraway seed

½ tablespoon chopped parsley leaves

Peperonata

This savory, slightly hot vegetable compote adds depth to sandwiches and wraps and makes a delicious omelette filling. It can also substitute as a side to replace cole slaw, pickles, or potato chips. The peperonata *(see photo on page 123)* can be made in advance and stored in an airtight container in the refrigerator for up to a week.

1. Heat the olive oil in a large sauté pan over medium heat. Add the onion and sauté until translucent, 4 to 5 minutes. Add the garlic, oregano, and red pepper flakes and sauté until aromatic, about 1 minute.

2. Add the green, red, and yellow peppers and continue to cook until the peppers are tender, 5 to 6 minutes more.

3. Stir in the parsley and thyme. Simmer over low heat until the mixture is flavorful, about 10 minutes. Season with the salt and black pepper. Serve warm or at room temperature.

Nutritional Information Per Serving: Calories 55, Protein 1 g, Carbohydrates 7.5 g, Fiber 2 g, Total Fat 3 g, Saturated Fat 0.5 g, Sodium 38 mg

MAKES 8 SERVINGS

1½ tablespoons extra-virgin olive oil

⅓ cup thinly sliced yellow onion

1 garlic clove, thinly sliced

¼ teaspoon dried oregano

¼ teaspoon red pepper flakes

2 cups thinly sliced green bell pepper

2 cups thinly sliced red bell pepper

2 cups thinly sliced yellow bell pepper

2 tablespoons chopped parsley leaves

2 teaspoons dried thyme

¼ teaspoon kosher salt

¼ teaspoon freshly ground black pepper

Fennel Salad with Blood Orange Vinaigrette

Blood oranges are in season during the winter months and three types dominate the market: Sanguinello (bull's blood), Moro, and Tarocco. The Moro has the deepest color flesh and shows the most red on the rind. The Sanquinello is similar to the Moro, but just a bit less bold and assertive. The Tarocco is considered the sweetest and best eating of the three. Any type of blood orange will work well for the vinaigrette. If you cannot find blood oranges, substitute regular oranges. You can also purchase an olive oil that is already infused with orange flavor to use in this recipe.

MAKES 2 SERVINGS

½ bulb fennel, thinly sliced

¼ red onion, thinly sliced

2 stalks celery, thinly sliced on the bias

4 parsley sprigs, leaves finely chopped

2 tablespoons fresh blood orange juice or regular orange juice

¼ teaspoon Dijon mustard

¼ teaspoon kosher salt

⅛ teaspoon freshly ground black pepper

1 tablespoon blood orange-infused olive oil

1. Mix together the fennel, onion, celery, and parsley.

2. Combine the orange juice, mustard, salt, and pepper. Whisk in the olive oil.

3. Drizzle the dressing over the vegetables and toss.

Nutritional Information Per Serving: Calories 104, Protein 1.5 g, Carbohydrates 10 g, Fiber 3.5 g, Total Fat 7 g, Saturated Fat 1 g, Sodium 252 mg

Steamed Kale with Cashews and Raspberries

Kale is such a hearty and versatile vegetable. The salty cashews and sweet and tart flavors from the raspberries contrast with the earthy kale. The lemon-infused olive oil can be found at most grocery stores.

1. Heat the olive oil in a sauté pan over medium high heat. Add the onion and cook until soft. Add the kale, wine, salt, and pepper. Cover and steam, 3 to 5 minutes.

2. While the kale is steaming, toss the raspberries with the vinegar and agave syrup.

3. When the kale is soft and most of the liquid has evaporated, add the cashews and raspberries. Cook until the raspberries are heated through and serve.

Nutritional Information Per Serving: Calories 98, Protein 2 g, Carbohydrates 9 g, Fiber 2 g, Total Fat 6 g, Saturated Fat 1 g, Sodium 139 mg

MAKES 4 SERVINGS

1½ tablespoons lemon-infused olive oil

½ small red onion, diced

6 cups packed kale leaves with stems removed

¼ cup white wine

½ teaspoon kosher salt

¼ teaspoon freshly ground black pepper

¾ cup raspberries

2 teaspoons balsamic vinegar

1 teaspoon agave syrup

3 tablespoons salted, roasted cashews, chopped

Sautéed Kale with Shallots

The Tuthill House at the Mill Restaurant & Tavern in Gardiner, New York, serves a side dish of kale that even people who don't like vegetables will enjoy. They kindly shared the recipe with me and I am so glad to pass it on. With hints of sweetness from the shallots and wine, it is an excellent way to add dark, leafy greens to a meal without any bitterness.

1. Blanch the kale leaves, then briefly immerse them in an ice bath to help set the bright green color. Roughly chop the kale into large pieces and set aside.

2. Heat the olive oil in a large sauté pan over medium high heat. Add the shallot and sauté until soft.

3. Add the kale, tossing to coat with the oil and mix with the shallots. Add the wine and bring to a boil. Cook until the volume of the wine is reduced by half. Season with the salt and pepper and serve.

Nutritional Information Per Serving: Calories 126, Protein 4 g, Carbohydrates 12 g, Fiber 2 g, Total Fat 6 g, Saturated Fat 1 g, Sodium 184 mg

MAKES 4 SERVINGS

1 large bunch kale, stems removed (makes about 6 cups of leaves once blanched and chopped)

1½ tablespoons olive oil

1 shallot, sliced

½ cup Sauvignon Blanc or other dry white wine

½ teaspoon kosher salt

¼ teaspoon freshly ground black pepper

Mushroom-Parmesan Salad

Raw mushrooms are sliced super thin in this salad and provide a refreshing change from sautéed mushrooms *(see photo on page 98).*

1. Combine the vinegar, shallots, salt, and pepper. Whisk in the olive oil.

2. Toss the dressing with the mushrooms, parsley, and Parmesan.

Nutritional Information Per Serving: Calories 139, Protein 3.5 g, Carbohydrates 2.5 g, Fiber 0 g, Total Fat 12.5 g, Saturated Fat 3 g, Sodium 284 mg

MAKES 2 SERVINGS

2 teaspoons sherry vinegar

1 tablespoon minced shallots

¼ teaspoon kosher salt

⅛ teaspoon freshly ground black pepper

4 teaspoons olive oil

6 large white mushrooms, thinly sliced

4 parsley sprigs, leaves removed and chopped

¾ ounce Parmesan, grated

Roasted Radishes

Roasting tempers the slightly bitter flavor of the radishes and brings out their natural sweetness. Give this technique a try in your kitchen to add to your repertoire of ways to serve radishes. See photo on page 126.

1. Preheat the oven to 450°F.

2. Toss the radishes with the canola oil, salt, and pepper.

3. Place the radishes cut side down on baking tray coated with cooking spray.

3. Roast until the sliced sides are golden brown and the radishes are soft, about 30 minutes. Remove from the oven and toss with the dressing and chives. Finish with ground black pepper to taste. Serve warm or at room temperature.

Nutritional Information Per Serving: Calories 33, Protein 0 g, Carbohydrates 4 g, Fiber 0.5 g, Total Fat 2 g, Saturated Fat 0 g, Sodium 184 mg

MAKES 4 SERVINGS

2 bunches red radishes, cleaned, tops removed and sliced in half

1 teaspoon canola oil

⅛ teaspoon kosher salt

⅛ teaspoon freshly ground black pepper, plus more to taste

¼ cup Ginger, Orange, and Sesame Dressing (recipe follows)

1 tablespoon chopped chives

Ginger, Orange, and Sesame Dressing

The ginger in this recipe gives the dressing a bit of a kick, which is offset by the sweetness of the orange juice and the bitterness of the orange zest.

1. Heat the sesame oil in a sauté pan over medium heat. Add the shallot, garlic, and ginger and sauté until soft. Add the orange zest and set aside.

2. Stir the arrowroot with 1 teaspoon of the chicken broth to form a paste. Bring the remaining broth, the orange juice, and vinegar to a boil.

3. Add the soy sauce and arrowroot paste. Allow the mixture to boil until thickened and reduced slightly, stirring constantly. Remove from the heat and whisk in the salt, pepper, and reserved ginger mixture. Use warm as a sauce or allow to cool and use as a dressing.

Nutritional Information Per Tablespoon: Calories 16, Protein 0 g, Carbohydrates 2 g, Fiber 0 g, Total Fat 1 g, Saturated Fat 0 g, Sodium 110 mg

MAKES 1 CUP

1 tablespoon pure sesame oil

2 tablespoons minced shallots

1 garlic clove, minced

1 tablespoon minced ginger

2 teaspoons orange zest

¾ teaspoon arrowroot

¾ cup low-sodium chicken broth

¼ cup fresh orange juice

¼ cup rice wine vinegar

1 tablespoon reduced-sodium soy sauce

½ teaspoon kosher salt

½ teaspoon freshly ground black pepper

Daikon Radish–Sesame Salad

Look for clean, white, firm daikons that are heavy for their size. Avoid those that are sallow in color and showing signs of dehydration or discoloration. Daikons that are oversized may be slightly woody or fibrous, so try to select one that is small to medium in size.

1. Combine the radish and cilantro.

2. Mix the orange zest with the sesame oil. Whisk in the orange juice and vinegar. Add the salt, pepper, and cayenne.

3. Add the sesame seeds to the radish mixture. Drizzle the dressing over the top and toss.

Nutritional Information Per Serving: Calories 66, Protein 1.5 g, Carbohydrates 5 g, Fiber 1.5 g, Total Fat 5 g, Saturated Fat 0.5 g, Sodium 22 mg

MAKES 4 SERVINGS

1 daikon radish, peeled and julienned

1 small bunch cilantro, chopped

1 orange, zested and 2 tablespoons fresh juice reserved

2 teaspoons sesame oil

2 tablespoons rice wine vinegar

¼ teaspoon kosher salt

¼ teaspoons freshly ground black pepper

⅛ teaspoon cayenne

2 tablespoons sesame seeds, toasted

Jícama and Red Pepper Salad

Jícama is a large, round, heavy tuber with thin, brown skin and crisp, crunchy, mildly sweet flesh. Although jícama is typically served raw, as it is here, it can also be sautéed without losing its texture.

1. To make the dressing, combine the lime juice, agave syrup, Tabasco, salt, and pepper. Add the canola oil in a steady stream, whisking constantly.

2. Add the jícama, red pepper, green onions, cilantro, and garlic to the dressing.

3. Cover the salad and marinate in the refrigerator for at least 30 minutes and up to 3 days before serving. Serve the salad chilled or at room temperature.

Nutritional Information Per Serving: Calories 108, Protein 0.5 g, Carbohydrates 11 g, Fiber 4.5 g, Total Fat 7 g, Saturated Fat 0.5 g, Sodium 80 mg

MAKES 8 SERVINGS

3 tablespoons fresh lime juice (about 2 limes)

2 teaspoons agave syrup

1 teaspoons Tabasco sauce

½ teaspoon kosher salt

¼ teaspoon freshly ground black pepper

¼ cup canola oil

1 medium jícama, peeled and julienned

1 large red bell pepper, julienned

2 green onions, thinly sliced on the bias

2 tablespoons chopped cilantro

2 teaspoons minced garlic

Spinach and White Beans with Ginger, Orange, and Sesame Dressing

For a different variation, try this dish mixed with the Italian "Sausage" Vinaigrette on page 142.

MAKES 4 SERVINGS

¼ cup low-sodium chicken broth

8 cups baby spinach leaves

½ cup cooked white beans

⅛ teaspoon kosher salt

⅛ teaspoon freshly ground black pepper

¼ cup Ginger, Orange, and Sesame Dressing (page 156)

1. Heat a skillet over medium high. Add the chicken broth and spinach. Allow the spinach to wilt and the broth to reduce slightly.

2. Stir in the beans, salt, and pepper and cook to reduce the broth by at least half the volume.

3. Toss the spinach mixture with the dressing and serve.

Nutritional Information Per Serving: Calories 68, Protein 4 g, Carbohydrates 13 g, Fiber 4 g, Total Fat 1 g, Saturated Fat 0 g, Sodium 285 mg

Sugar Snap Peas with Champagne Vinaigrette

The simple flavors of the vinaigrette allow the fresh, grassy, herbaceous flavors of the sugar snap peas to shine through *(see photo page 100)*. Try to find the freshest sugar snap peas possible. Definitely make a stop at your local farm stand if you can.

1. Blanch the sugar snap peas to bring out their bright green color.

2. Dry with a paper towel.

3. Toss with the vinaigrette and serve warm. To serve cold, immerse the blanched snap peas in an ice water bath to stop cooking, and then toss with vinaigrette.

Nutritional Information Per Serving: Calories 60, Protein 1 g, Carbohydrates 4 g, Fiber 1 g, Total Fat 5 g, Saturated Fat 0.5 g, Sodium 14 mg

MAKES 2 SERVINGS

1 pint sugar snap peas

1 tablespoon Champagne Vinaigrette (recipe follows)

Champagne Vinaigrette

This basic vinaigrette is great with other light, subtle herbs too—try marjoram, savory, thyme, or oregano.

Combine the vinegar, herbs, salt, and pepper. Whisk in the olive oil.

Nutritional Information Per Tablespoon: Calories 83 , Protein 0 g, Carbohydrates 0.5 g, Fiber 0 g, Total Fat 9 g, Saturated Fat 1 g, Sodium 23 mg

MAKES ABOUT 1½ CUPS

½ cup champagne vinegar

2 teaspoons minced garlic

1 tablespoon chopped parsley

½ teaspoon kosher salt

Freshly ground black pepper, to taste

1 cup extra-virgin olive oil

Pan-Steamed Zucchini and Yellow Squash Noodles

These squash "noodles" are so versatile—try them with other herbs such as basil, tarragon, chives, cilantro, thyme, or oregano. You can also mix them with some spaghetti or fettucine, but count the extra carbohydrates added by the pasta.

1. Using a mandoline or a julienne peeler, slice the zucchini and squash lengthwise into ¼-inch-thick "noodles." Discard the center of the squashes with the seeds.

2. Heat the butter in a sauté pan over medium high heat. Add the shallot and garlic and sweat until the shallot is translucent.

3. Add the squash noodles and the vegetable or chicken broth to the sauté pan. Cover and pan-steam until tender, about 3 minutes. Drain any excess liquid. Season with the herbs, lemon juice, salt, and pepper.

Nutritional Information Per Serving: Calories 56, Protein 2.5 g, Carbohydrates 7.5 g, Fiber 1.5 g, Total Fat 2.5 g, Saturated Fat 1.5 g, Sodium 137 mg

MAKES 2 SERVINGS

2 small zucchini

2 small yellow squash

1 teaspoon butter

½ shallot, minced

1 garlic clove, minced

3 tablespoons vegetable *or* chicken broth

1 tablespoon minced herbs

1 teaspoon fresh lemon juice

⅛ teaspoon kosher salt

⅛ teaspoon freshly ground black pepper

Peel the zucchini with a julienne peeler to make thin "noodles."

Zucchini-Mushroom Griddlecakes

Any salt-free, dried herb mixture can be used in these savory griddlecakes. Serve them with extra sautéed mushrooms on top if desired. For a homemade version of the whole wheat instant baking mix, see the Apple Walnut Biscuits on page 185.

1. Heat the olive oil in a sauté pan over medium high heat. Add the mushrooms and sweat. When they have released some of their liquid, stir in the onion and cook until the onion is soft and translucent and mushrooms have released most of their liquid. Remove from the heat and stir in the zucchini. Set aside to cool.

2. Preheat a nonstick griddle to medium (about 300°F).

3. Combine the baking mix, salt, sugar, and herb mix. Whisk together the egg and buttermilk. Add to the dry mixture and mix to combine. Stir in the zucchini mixture.

4. Use a half-cup scoop or ladle to portion out the batter onto the nonstick griddle. Cook on both sides until golden brown. Top with the grated cheese and serve.

Nutritional Information Per Griddlecake: Calories 54, Protein 3 g, Carbohydrates 4 g, Fiber 0.5 g, Total Fat 3 g, Saturated Fat 1 g, Sodium 69 mg

MAKES 9 GRIDDLECAKES

2 teaspoons olive oil

1 cup sliced cremini mushrooms

½ yellow onion, diced

1 medium zucchini, shredded

1 cup whole wheat instant baking mix

½ teaspoon kosher salt

1 tablespoon sugar

2 teaspoons Parisian fines herb mix (chives, dill, basil, tarragon, chervil)

¾ cup buttermilk

1 egg

1 ounce grated hard cheese (Parmesan works well)

Chayote Salad with Oranges

Chayote, a member of the squash family, is relatively soft skinned. Its mild flavor and crisp texture make it great for salads.

1. Mix the chayote, jícama, carrots, orange sections, and green onions to combine.

2. Combine the olive oil, lime juice, sugar, salt, pepper, and reserved orange juice. Drizzle the dressing over the vegetables.

3. Add the cilantro and mint, and toss to combine.

Nutritional Information Per Serving: Calories 130, Protein 2 g, Carbohydrates 17 g, Fiber 6 g, Total Fat 7 g, Saturated Fat 1 g, Sodium 120 mg

MAKES 4 SERVINGS

1 chayote, peeled and thinly sliced

2 cups peeled, thinly sliced jícama

2 cups thinly sliced carrot

2 oranges, peeled and sectioned, juices reserved

½ bunch green onions, thinly sliced

2 tablespoons extra-virgin olive oil

2 tablespoons fresh lime juice

¾ teaspoon sugar

¼ teaspoon kosher salt

¼ teaspoon freshly ground black pepper

2 tablespoons chopped cilantro

2 tablespoons chopped mint

String Beans with Almonds

The classic string beans almandine uses butter and lemon juice. We swapped out the butter for almond oil and used white wine in place of the lemon juice. The results are a delicious twist on the original dish.

1. Steam the string beans just until tender and set aside.

2. Heat the almond oil in a sauté pan over medium heat. Add the almonds and sauté until lightly brown.

3. Add the cooked beans and toss to coat. Add the white wine and bring to a boil. Cook until the volume of the wine is reduced by half. Season with the salt and serve.

Nutritional Information Per Serving: Calories 103, Protein 3 g, Carbohydrates 9 g, Fiber 3.5 g, Total Fat 5 g, Saturated Fat 0.5 g, Sodium 76 mg

MAKES 4 SERVINGS

4 cups green string beans, ends removed

1½ teaspoons almond oil

¼ cup sliced almonds

¼ cup white wine

¼ teaspoon kosher or sea salt

Edamame with Tarragon Dipping Sauce

Edamame can be used like green peas in many dishes, or they can be boiled and salted. We serve them with a tarragon dipping sauce and they become rather addictive. Eat them by dipping the bean in the sauce and then putting the whole pod in your mouth while holding on to the end of the pod. Gently pull the pod through your teeth and the beans pop out into your mouth. Discard the pod and move onto the next one.

MAKES 4 SERVINGS

6 cups water

½ teaspoon kosher salt

4 cups edamame in pods (frozen or fresh)

½ cup Tarragon Dipping Sauce (recipe follows)

1. Bring the water to a boil and add the salt.

2. Boil the edamame until beans are tender, 4 to 5 minutes. Drain and serve with the dipping sauce.

Nutritional Information Per Serving: Calories 238, Protein 16 g, Carbohydrates 18 g, Fiber 8 g, Total Fat 10 g, Saturated Fat 0.5 g, Sodium 154 mg

Tarragon Dipping Sauce

This flavorful dipping sauce is also delicious with grilled meats and fish.

MAKES ¾ CUP

¾ teaspoon arrowroot

½ cup low-sodium chicken broth

¼ cup white wine vinegar

½ teaspoon Dijon mustard

¼ teaspoon kosher salt

¼ teaspoon freshly ground black pepper

1 teaspoon minced tarragon

1 teaspoon minced shallot

1 teaspoon minced garlic

¼ cup olive oil

1. Dissolve the arrowroot in 1 tablespoon of the chicken broth to make a paste. Bring the remaining broth to a boil.

2. Stir the paste into the broth and allow the broth to thicken slightly. Remove from the heat and add the vinegar, mustard, salt, pepper, tarragon, shallot, and garlic.

3. Whisk in the olive oil.

Nutritional Information Per Tablespoon: Calories 38, Protein 0 g, Carbohydrates 0 g, Fiber 0 g, Total Fat 4.5 g, Saturated Fat 0.5 g, Sodium 25 mg

Hearts of Artichoke Salad

Artichoke hearts are tender and delicious and pair perfectly with the sharp red onion, briny kalamata olives, and sweet tomatoes.

1. Defrost the frozen artichoke hearts or cut the ends off the fresh artichokes and trim off the outer leaves. Scoop out the chokes. Quarter each heart and rub with the lemon halves. Hold the hearts in water mixed with lemon juice from one lemon half.

2. In a large pot, simmer the artichoke hearts in fresh water until tender, 8 to 12 minutes. Drain and dry on paper towels while preparing the dressing.

3. Whisk the olive oil, vinegar, salt, pepper, and parsley to combine. Add the artichoke hearts, olives, onion, and tomatoes, and toss to combine.

4. Let rest at room temperature for at least 30 minutes before serving.

Nutritional Information Per Serving: Calories 108, Protein 1 g, Carbohydrates 7 g, Fiber 1.5 g, Total Fat 9 g, Saturated Fat 1 g, Sodium 203 mg

MAKES 4 SERVINGS

4 fresh or frozen artichoke hearts

1 lemon, halved

2 tablespoons olive oil

2½ teaspoons balsamic vinegar

¼ teaspoon kosher salt

¼ teaspoon white pepper

¼ cup parsley leaves, chopped

8 kalamata olives, pitted and chopped

½ red onion, thinly sliced

4 plum tomatoes, peeled, seeded, and quartered

Remove the top and excess stem of the artichoke.

Trim away the tough outer leaves with a paring knife.

Scoop out the choke to finish cleaning the heart.

Roasted Carrots and Celeriac with Fennel Seeds

Celeriac is a versatile vegetable that is grown around the world and can be boiled or roasted and served in soups, stews, and side dishes. This makes a nice side dish for the Caraway-Herb Roasted Pork Tenderloin *(page 123)*. This recipe can be doubled or tripled and you can enjoy the leftovers for another meal.

1. Preheat the oven to 450°F.

2. Toss together the celeriac, carrots, olive oil, salt, pepper, and fennel seeds.

3. Place the vegetables on a greased baking sheet and roast, turning the vegetables halfway through the cooking so all sides are well browned, about 40 minutes.

Nutritional Information Per Serving: Calories 78, Protein 1.5 g, Carbohydrates 10 g, Fiber 3 g, Total Fat 4 g, Saturated Fat 0.5 g, Sodium 125 mg

MAKES 2 SERVINGS

½ medium celeriac cut into batonnets about ½ inch thick and 2 inches long (about 2 cups)

½ pound carrots cut into batonnets about ½ inch thick and 2 inches long

1 tablespoon olive oil

⅛ teaspoon kosher salt

⅛ teaspoon freshly ground black pepper

1 tablespoon fennel seed

Tomato, Parsley, and Feta Salad

This salad is light, fresh, and tasty all at the same time. If you can't find lemon-infused olive oil, substitute with extra-virgin olive oil or you can infuse your own olive oil by simmering lemon zest in the oil for about 30 minutes.

MAKES 6 SERVINGS

8 plum tomatoes

½ small red onion, diced

1 cup chopped parsley

1 ounce feta, crumbled

2 tablespoons fresh lemon juice, plus more to taste

1 teaspoon agave syrup

½ teaspoon kosher salt

½ teaspoon freshly ground black pepper, plus more to taste

1½ tablespoons lemon-infused olive oil

1. Cut the plum tomatoes into eighths and remove the seeds. Mix together the tomatoes, onion, parsley, and feta.

2. Mix together the lemon juice, agave syrup, salt, and pepper. Whisk in the olive oil. Toss the dressing with the tomato mixture. Finish with a squeeze of fresh lemon juice and a grind of black pepper just before serving.

Nutritional Information Per Serving: Calories 68, Protein 2 g, Carbohydrates 6 g, Fiber 1.5 g, Total Fat 4.5 g, Saturated Fat 1 g, Sodium 150 mg

Broccoli and Brussels Sprout Slaw

The stalks of the broccoli are used to make this slaw. The shredded Brussels sprouts blend in with the carrots and broccoli so even if you're not a fan of Brussels sprouts you can enjoy their goodness in this recipe.

1. For the dressing, whisk together the vinegar, agave syrup, salt, and celery seeds. Set aside.

2. Peel the tough outer layer of the broccoli stalks and cut into two-inch-long sections. Cut the sections into thin, julienned strips. You will have about 1½ cups when done.

4. Slice the Brussels sprouts crosswise into ⅛-inch-thick strips. You will have about 1½ cups when done.

5. Blanch the broccoli and Brussels sprout pieces in boiling water for about 30 seconds until bright green. Immerse in ice water to cool. Drain well.

6. Mix the carrots, broccoli, and Brussels sprouts with the dressing. Toss with the sunflower seeds and currants and serve.

Nutritional Information Per Serving: Calories 62, Protein 2.5 g, Carbohydrates 10 g, Fiber 2.5 g, Total Fat 2 g, Saturated Fat 0 g, Sodium 114 mg

MAKES 4 SERVINGS

1 tablespoon rice wine vinegar

2 teaspoons agave syrup

¼ teaspoon kosher salt

½ teaspoon celery seed

2 stalks broccoli

4 large Brussels sprouts

1 large carrot, peeled and cut into 2-inch julienned strips (about 1 cup)

2 tablespoons dry roasted sunflower seeds

1 tablespoon zante currants

Spaghetti Squash with Rosemary and Walnuts

The long strands of pale flesh that are scraped from the roasted squash resemble spaghetti strands and add a different texture to the repertoire of vegetable sides. Roasting instead of steaming the squash concentrates the flavor and adds a hint of sweetness to the dish.

1. Preheat the oven to 450°F.

2. Place the squash halves in a small roasting pan with cut side up. Roast, uncovered, for 1 hour.

3. While the squash is roasting, toast the walnuts in the oven for about 10 minutes until golden brown. Check on the walnuts after 5 minutes and watch closely so they do not burn.

4. Run the tines of a fork lengthwise through the flesh of the roasted squash to create long strands. Toss the squash strands with the salt and pepper. Hold in the hot oven.

5. Heat the olive oil over medium high heat in a heavy sauté pan. Sauté the red onion with the rosemary until soft and translucent. Add the white wine and allow to reduce by half.

6. Add the roasted squash and walnuts to the sauté pan with the onions and mix well and serve.

Nutritional Information Per Serving: Calories 118, Protein 2 g, Carbohydrates 9.5 g, Fiber 2.5 g, Total Fat 9 g, Saturated Fat 1 g, Sodium 113 mg

MAKES 6 SERVINGS

1 spaghetti squash, sliced in half lengthwise and seeds removed

½ cup chopped walnuts

½ teaspoon kosher salt

¼ teaspoon freshly ground black pepper

1 tablespoon olive oil

½ cup chopped red onion

1 teaspoon dried rosemary leaves, crushed

¼ cup white wine

Irish Latkes

This is a variation of Ireland's traditional potato dish, colcannon, prepared in the tradition of Jewish potato latkes. It is diabetes-friendly because mashed calypso or snowcap "potato" beans are used in place of shredded or mashed potatoes, adding more fiber and protein. Grated cauliflower is added in place of the cabbage often used in true colcannon since it has a milder flavor.

1. Preheat the oven to 400°F.

2. Mash together the beans and chicken broth. Stir in the cauliflower, chives, ½ teaspoon of the salt, the pepper, eggs, and flour.

3. Heat the canola oil in a heavy skillet over medium high heat until very hot but not smoking. Drop the bean mixture in ½-cup portions into the hot oil and flatten slightly with a spatula.

4. Fry until golden brown, about 1 minute per side. Transfer to a baking sheet. Repeat with the remaining bean mixture, making sure to let the pan heat up again between batches.

5. Continue cooking in the oven for 10 minutes more. Sprinkle with the remaining ¼ teaspoon salt and serve.

Note The nutritional analysis is based on a total weight 3 ounces of oil being absorbed.

Nutritional Information Per Latke: Calories 181, Protein 6 g, Carbohydrates 14 g, Fiber 4 g, Total Fat 12 g, Saturated Fat 1 g, Sodium 128 mg

MAKES 8 SERVINGS

2 cups cooked calypso or snowcap beans

¼ cup low-sodium chicken broth

1 cup grated raw cauliflower

3 tablespoons minced chives

¾ teaspoon kosher salt

¼ teaspoon freshly ground black pepper

2 eggs, lightly beaten

2 tablespoons whole wheat flour

1 cup canola oil, for frying

Lentil and Parsley Salad with Mustard-Sherry Vinaigrette

The earthiness of the mustard and lentils in this salad pairs beautifully with Gamay Noir from Whitecliff Vineyard in New York State's Hudson Valley *(see photo on page 122)*.

1. Soak the lentils in the water for several hours until they absorb some of the water, soften, and expand in size.

2. Drain the lentils and transfer to a heavy stockpot. Add the vegetable broth and ½ teaspoon of the salt. Tie the whole garlic clove, the peppercorns, bay leaf, parsley, and thyme in cheesecloth to make a sachet and add to the stockpot.

3. Bring to a boil, reduce the heat and simmer, covered, until soft, 25 to 30 minutes. Do not overcook the lentils or they will lose their shape. Remove the lentils from the cooking liquid. Toss the lentils with 1 tablespoon of the walnut oil and spread them out on a sheet tray to cool.

4. Heat the remaining 1 tablespoon walnut oil in a sauté pan over medium heat. Add the onion and sauté until soft and it begins to caramelize. Add the onion to the cooked lentils and allow to cool.

5. While the lentils and onions cool, prepare the vinaigrette. Mix the vinegar, mustard, shallot, the remaining ½ teaspoon salt, the pepper, and sugar. Gradually whisk in the olive oil.

6. Transfer the lentil mixture to a bowl and add the parsley. Drizzle the dressing over the salad and toss. This salad holds well and is delicious several days after preparation.

Nutritional Information Per Serving: Calories 308, Protein 13 g, Carbohydrates 40 g, Fiber 10 g, Total Fat 12 g, Saturated Fat 1 g, Sodium 250 mg

MAKES 8 SERVINGS

1 pound dried lentils

2 quarts water

1 quart vegetable broth

1 teaspoon kosher salt

2 garlic cloves, 1 whole and 1 minced

4 black peppercorns

1 bay leaf

2 parsley sprigs

2 thyme sprigs

2 tablespoons walnut oil

1 large onion, diced

1 tablespoon sherry vinegar

2 teaspoons Dijon mustard

½ shallot, minced

½ teaspoon freshly ground black pepper

1 teaspoon brown sugar

¼ cup olive oil

1 cup chopped Italian parsley

Black-eyed Pea Salad

Black-eyed peas make this South American–influenced salad unique and out of the ordinary. See photo on page 100.

1. In a large pot, cover the black-eyed peas with water, bring to a boil then reduce the heat and simmer the peas until tender, 10 to 15 minutes. Drain well.

2. In a large sauté pan, heat the olive oil over medium heat. Add the onions, garlic, and ginger and cook until the onions are translucent, 4 to 5 minutes

3. Add the curry and turmeric and cook until fragrant, 1 to 2 minutes more.

4. Stir in the black-eyed peas, corn, thyme, vinegar, lime juice, sesame oil, salt, and pepper. Continue cooking until the mixture is heated through, then remove from the heat and cool to room temperature.

5. Transfer the mixture to a large bowl, and toss with the tomatoes, green onions, and cilantro. Let sit for 15 to 20 minutes so that the flavors can combine.

Nutritional Information Per Serving: Calories 237, Protein 11 g, Carbohydrates 34 g, Fiber 6 g, Total Fat 7 g, Saturated Fat 1 g, Sodium 197 mg

MAKES 8 SERVINGS

2 cups dried black-eyed peas, soaked overnight

3 tablespoons olive oil

1 cup minced onion

2 garlic cloves, minced

1 teaspoon minced ginger

1 tablespoon curry powder

1 teaspoon ground turmeric

1 cup corn kernels

½ teaspoon minced thyme

1 tablespoon rice wine vinegar

1 lime, juiced

1½ teaspoons sesame oil

½ teaspoon kosher salt

¼ teaspoon freshly ground black pepper

2 cups diced, seeded tomatoes

1 bunch green onions, thinly sliced

¼ cup chopped cilantro

Smashed Calypso Beans and Butter

I like to call this heirloom bean the *potato bean* because they taste more like potatoes than beans! Another heirloom bean that reminds me of red skin potatoes is the snowcap bean. Heirloom beans often cook more quickly than the beans found at the grocery store. Both can be purchased online from companies that sell a variety of heirloom beans. *(See photo on page 124 and the appendix on page 219 for website sources.)*

MAKES 6 SERVINGS

8 ounces dried calypso beans

½ teaspoon kosher salt

2 tablespoons unsalted butter

¼ teaspoon freshly ground black pepper

2 tablespoons snipped chives

1. Soak the beans overnight or up to 2 days in water in the refrigerator. (If you forget to do this step you can still proceed with the recipe but the cooking time will be longer.) Drain the beans and rinse.

2. Transfer the beans to a soup pot with a lid and add 6 cups fresh water and the salt. Bring to a boil, reduce the heat, and simmer slowly, covered, until the beans are very tender, 30 to 40 minutes.

3. Drain the beans, add the butter, and mash with a spoon. Allow some of the beans to remain whole, if desired. Sprinkle with the pepper and chives and serve.

Nutritional Information Per Serving: Calories 196, Protein 10 g, Carbohydrates 30 g, Fiber 10 g, Total Fat 4.5 g, Saturated Fat 3 g, Sodium 141 mg

Barley and Couscous Pilaf

This pilaf *(see photo page 103)* is a versatile side dish and is great with the Chicken Kebabs with Mint-Parsley Pesto *(page 34)*. Whole wheat Israeli couscous works well in this recipe because the grains are larger and mix well with the barley.

1. Heat the olive oil in saucepan over medium high heat. Add the celery and onion and sweat until soft. Add the cumin and the barley and toast lightly.

2. Add 1½ cups of the chicken broth, salt, and pepper and bring to a boil. Reduce the heat and simmer, covered, until barley is tender but not mushy, about 1 hour. During the last 5 minutes of cooking, bring the remaining 1 cup broth to a boil in a small saucepan and add the couscous.

3. Reduce heat and simmer the couscous, covered, until al dente, about 5 minutes.

4. Mix the barley and couscous together and serve.

Note The barley can be made in large quantities in advance. Cool down and freeze in half-cup portions. Stir frozen barley into the couscous just as it finishes cooking to heat barley through.

Nutritional Information Per Serving: Calories 130, Protein 5 g, Carbohydrates 25 g, Fiber 5 g, Total Fat 1 g, Saturated Fat 0 g, Sodium 134 mg

MAKES 6 SERVINGS

1 teaspoon olive oil

1 stalk celery, diced

½ medium yellow onion, diced

1 teaspoon ground cumin

½ cup pearled barley

2½ cups low-sodium chicken broth

½ teaspoon kosher salt

¼ teaspoon freshly ground black pepper

½ cup whole wheat Israeli couscous

Mixed-Grain Pilaf

This pilaf can be made with a mixture of any of your favorite whole grains *(see photo on page 104).* If you are hesitant to try a new whole grain consider mixing it with more familiar starches like white rice. As you become accustomed to the unique flavors and textures of the whole grains you can start to change the ratio and eventually you may prefer 100% of the whole grain.

1. Heat the olive oil in a large pot over medium high heat. Add the onions and celery and sweat until soft. Add the wheat berries, rice, barley, and vegetable broth, salt, and pepper and bring to a boil over medium heat.

2. Simmer, covered, over low heat until the grains are soft and the liquid is absorbed, about 1 hour.

Nutritional Information Per Serving: Calories 150, Protein 5 g, Carbohydrates 28 g, Fiber 4 g, Total Fat 1 g, Saturated Fat 0 g, Sodium 139 mg

MAKES 8 SERVINGS

1 teaspoon olive oil

½ cup minced onion

½ cup minced celery

½ cup wheat berries

½ cup wild rice

½ cup pearled barley

6¾ cups vegetable or low-sodium chicken broth

½ teaspoon kosher salt

¼ teaspoon freshly ground black pepper

Desserts and Baked Goods

Sugar, flour, butter, cream, eggs—the delicious basic ingredients of so many desserts and baked goods. They make an enticing combo that challenges us to stay in control of the amount we eat. Many people with diabetes believe low sugar or sugar-free sweets are better choices. This is not necessarily the case. Artificial sweeteners such as aspartame, sucralose, and plant extracts such as stevia are not magic ingredients that create diabetes-friendly desserts. Although these sweeteners are calorie and carbohydrate-free, they are rarely used alone. They team up with refined starches, like white flour, that contains very little fiber and can result in a rapid rise in your blood glucose level. Frequently the fats of choice in desserts are saturated fats like butter and cream which can contribute to an increase in the bad (LDL) cholesterol in your blood if consumed in large amounts. Even the sugar substitutes such as xylitol, sorbitol, and maltitol are not a free pass to dessert heaven since they contain some carbohydrate and calories. Go overboard on these sugar substitutes and they may remind you of your indulgence with their laxative effects.

Desserts and sweets are meant to be a treat in everyone's diet since they usually do not provide loads of nutrients or health-promoting substances like antioxidants. In this chapter you will find recipes that require some self-control because they are high in fat and carbohydrates and you will find some that are easier to fit into a meal plan since they contain smaller amounts of butter, shortening or lard and include more health promoting ingredients like whole grain oats, omega-3 rich nut oils, and antioxidant-rich fruits.

Ultimately you must be honest with yourself and monitor your blood glucose response to having these treats around your house or as part of a special meal. Remember, that if you eat too much of a "healthy" treat like the Dark Chocolate-Glazed Oatmeal Cookies on page 191, you will still end up with high blood glucose levels or weight gain and there is nothing healthy about that. Therefore, portion control always remains important. This becomes easier when your treat has a clear beginning and ending. A whole layer cake or pie invites repeated tasting which can add unwanted carbohydrates, fat and calories. So mini dessert recipes are intentionally included to help you enjoy them without over-indulging.

Barley Buttermilk Flatbread

Zatar seasoning is a popular Middle Eastern spice blend of ground sumac berries, thyme, sesame seeds, and salt. Sumac adds a slightly fruity tang to the spice mix that blends well with the buttermilk.

MAKES 8 SERVINGS

½ cup plus 2 tablespoons barley flour

½ cup plus 2 tablespoons white whole wheat flour

1 teaspoon brown sugar

¾ teaspoon baking powder

¼ teaspoon baking soda

2 teaspoons zatar seasoning

½ teaspoon kosher salt

½ cup buttermilk

2 tablespoons olive oil

1. Preheat the oven to 425°F. Coat a baking sheet with nonstick cooking spray.

2. Combine the barley and whole wheat flours, the brown sugar, baking powder, baking soda, 1 teaspoon of the zatar, and the salt. Stir with a fork to mix well. Stir in the buttermilk and 5 teaspoons of the olive oil and mix until smooth.

3. Dust a cutting board with flour and turn the dough out onto it. Pat the dough into a circle about ¼ inch thick. Top with the remaining 1 teaspoon olive oil and 1 teaspoon zatar seasoning. Cut into 8 wedges and place on the prepared baking sheet. Bake until golden brown, about 15 minutes.

Nutritional Information Per Serving: Calories 116, Protein 3 g, Carbohydrates 16 g, Fiber 3 g, Total Fat 4 g, Saturated Fat 1 g, Sodium 187 mg

Orange Oatmeal Muffins

White whole wheat flour is made from whole-grain wheat so it provides the fiber and nutritional benefits associated with whole grains. However, it is a different variety of wheat and, therefore, does not taste as earthy as some whole wheat flours.

1. Combine the buttermilk, oats, and vanilla. Chill overnight.

2. Preheat the oven to 400°F.

3. Coat a 12-cup muffin tin with cooking spray. Mix the canola oil and orange zest in a small pan and bring to a simmer for 3 minutes to allow the orange flavor to infuse the oil. Remove from heat and allow to cool to room temperature.

4. Beat the eggs. Add the sucralose–brown sugar blend and beat until smooth.

5. Add the oats mixture, flour, baking soda, salt, ginger, orange-infused oil, and agave syrup.

6. Mix until the batter is well combined. Fill each muffin cup two-thirds to three-quarters full and bake for 20 minutes.

Nutritional Information Per Muffin: Calories 194, Protein 7 g, Carbohydrates 29 g, Fiber 3 g, Total Fat 5 g, Saturated Fat 1 g, Sodium 244 mg

MAKES 12 MUFFINS

1¾ cups plus 2 tablespoons low-fat buttermilk

1 cup steel-cut oats

1 teaspoon vanilla extract

2 tablespoons canola oil

1 teaspoon orange zest

2 eggs

6 tablespoons sucralose–brown sugar blend

1⅔ cups white whole wheat flour

1 teaspoon baking soda

1 teaspoon kosher salt

½ teaspoon ground ginger

2 tablespoons agave syrup

Apple Walnut Biscuits

This biscuit bakes up around an apple filling to make the biscuit very moist. Serve it with a little bit of apple butter if you like. If you have a favorite whole wheat baking mix that is available at your nearby grocery, simply substitute an equal amount of that baking mix.

1. For the whole wheat baking mix: Mix all the ingredients together and store in an airtight container. This can be stored to up to 6 months.

2. Preheat the oven to 400°F.

3. For the biscuits: Combine the baking mix, 1 teaspoon of the cinnamon, and the brown sugar in a food processor.

4. Cut the cold butter blend into the flour by pulsing the food processor. Add the milk and pulse until combined.

5. Turn dough out onto a board dusted with baking mix and knead dough lightly.

6. Cut the dough into 12 pieces and place each piece of dough into a greased muffin cup.

7. Mix the apples with the ginger, cloves, allspice, 1 teaspoon of the cinnamon, the salt, vanilla extract, agave syrup, and walnuts. Make a depression in the center of each piece of dough and fill with 2 to 3 tablespoons apple filling.

8. Bake for 12 minutes until biscuits are lightly brown.

9. Mix together the remaining cinnamon and confectioners' sugar and dust the tops of biscuits.

Nutritional Information Per Biscuit: Calories 200, Protein 4 g, Carbohydrates 29 g, Fiber 3 g, Total Fat 8.5 g, Saturated Fat 2 g, Sodium 302 mg

Nutritional Information Per Cup of Whole Wheat Baking Mix: Calories 315, Protein 10 g, Carbohydrates 64 g, Fiber 9.5 g, Total Fat 2 g, Saturated Fat 0.5 g, Sodium 1284 mg

MAKES 12 BISCUITS

WHOLE WHEAT BAKING MIX

2¼ cups whole wheat pastry flour

5¼ teaspoons baking powder

1¼ teaspoons Morton table salt

4½ teaspoons sugar

¼ cup buttermilk powder

APPLE WALNUT BISCUITS

2 cups Whole Wheat Baking Mix (recipe above)

1 tablespoon ground cinnamon

2 tablespoons brown sugar

2 tablespoons butter/vegetable oil blend (no trans fat), chilled

⅔ cup nonfat milk

4 apples, peeled, cored, and diced

¼ teaspoon ground ginger

¼ teaspoon ground cloves

¼ teaspoon ground allspice

½ teaspoon kosher salt

½ teaspoon vanilla extract

3 tablespoons agave syrup

1 cup chopped walnuts, toasted

1 tablespoon confectioners' sugar

Chocolate Cappuccino Shortbread with Dark Chocolate Glaze

These shortbreads freeze well and are great with a cup of coffee or Earl Grey tea. They are a little higher in saturated fat but well worth the indulgence.

MAKES 30 COOKIES

8 ounces unsalted butter, soft

½ cup dark brown sugar, packed

2 cups all-purpose flour

¼ cup cocoa powder

1 teaspoon espresso powder

2 tablespoons cornstarch

2 tablespoons granulated sugar

3 tablespoons Dark Chocolate Glaze (page 188)

1. Preheat the oven to 350°F.

2. Line a 9 by 13-inch cake pan with parchment paper.

3. Cream the butter and sugar in a mixer until soft and smooth. Stir together the flour, cocoa, espresso powder, and cornstarch.

4. Add the flour mixture to the butter mixture and mix on low speed until the ingredients are incorporated and start to form a dough. Turn the dough out onto a lightly floured board and knead to smooth the dough, about 5 times.

5. Roll out the dough on a lightly floured surface to the size of the prepared pan. Transfer to the pan and press in evenly. Prick the shortbread with the tines of a fork to prevent shrinkage.

6. Bake in the center of the oven for 15 minutes. Rotate the pan and bake until very lightly browned, 15 minutes more.

7. Remove from the oven and sprinkle with the sugar. Allow to cool in the pan for 10 minutes, then cut into 30 bars. Cool completely in the pan.

8. Drizzle the glaze over the tops.

Nutritional Information Per Cookie: Calories 115, Protein 1 g, Carbohydrates 13 g, Fiber 0.5 g, Total Fat 6.5 g, Saturated Fat 4.5 g, Sodium 2 mg

Strawberries with Dark Chocolate Glaze and Pecans

Serving sliced strawberries with a glaze is much easier than coating individual berries in chocolate.

Spread the sliced berries on 4 small plates. Drizzle the chocolate glaze over the berries and sprinkle with the chopped pecans.

Nutritional Information Per Serving: Calories 121 g, Protein 1.5 g, Carbohydrates 15 g, Fiber 3 g, Total Fat 7 g, Saturated Fat 2 g, Sodium 5 mg

MAKES 4 SERVINGS

1 pound sliced strawberries

¼ cup Dark Chocolate Glaze (recipe below)

3 tablespoons chopped, toasted pecans

Dark Chocolate Glaze

This rich chocolate is only lightly sweetened and uses almond-cashew cream as a substitute for heavy cream, making it less sinful—but no less decadent!

Combine the ingredients in a double boiler and stir until melted and well mixed.

Nutritional Information Per Tablespoon: Calories 58, Protein 0.5 g, Carbohydrates 6 g, Fiber 0.5 g, Total Fat 3.5 g, Saturated Fat 2 g, Sodium 4 mg

MAKES 10 TABLESPOONS

3 ounces dark, bittersweet chocolate (60% cacao)

¼ cup almond-cashew cream

1 tablespoon agave syrup

Strawberry Mini Cobblers

Cobblers are basically just biscuit dough dropped on top of pie filling. I find cobblers are quicker to make than a pie and much easier to make into individual mini desserts to help with portion control. By making the biscuit dough with some almond meal and oatmeal I added more protein and fiber to further lower the glycemic impact of the dessert.

1. Preheat oven to 375° F

2. Sift together the flour, baking powder, sugar, and salt. Stir in the almond meal.

3. Cut the butter into the flour mixture until it forms a coarse meal. Stir in the oats.

4. Stir the vinegar, almond and vanilla extracts into the nonfat milk and set aside.

5. Mix the berries with the sugar, cornstarch, salt, and vanilla extract and vanilla bean scrapings. Divide strawberry mixture among 8 small ceramic baking dishes.

6. Add the milk mixture to the flour mixture and stir until just moist and a dough has formed. Top the berries with spoonfuls of the biscuit dough.

7. Bake for 15 minutes then add the sliced almonds to the top. Continue to bake for an additional 15 to 20 minutes until the filling is very hot and bubbling over and the topping is golden brown. Allow to cool fully so the filling thickens.

Nutritional Information Per Cobbler: Calories 227, Protein 5 g, Carbohydrates 30 g, Fiber 3.5 g, Total Fat 11 g, Saturated Fat 4.5 g, Sodium 200 mg

MAKES 8 SERVINGS

BISCUITS

½ cup all-purpose flour (white whole wheat flour can also be used)

1 teaspoon baking powder

2 tablespoons sugar

½ teaspoon kosher salt

½ cup almond meal

½ stick unsalted butter (no–trans fat butter blend can also be used)

½ cup old-fashioned oats

½ teaspoon balsamic vinegar

½ teaspoon vanilla extract

½ teaspoon almond extract

½ cup nonfat milk

STRAWBERRIES

4 cups hulled strawberries, cut in half if large

½ cup sugar

1 tablespoon cornstarch

½ teaspoon kosher salt

½ teaspoon vanilla extract

1 vanilla bean cut in half and center scraped out *(optional)*

¼ cup sliced toasted almonds

Brown Sugar Crisps

A combination of regular brown sugar, agave syrup, and sucralose artificial sweeteners create a sweet cookie without a bitter aftertaste or excessive carbohydrates. You can crumble these cookies for a crispy topping on low-sugar ice cream and top with a drizzle of the Dark Chocolate Glaze *(page 188)*. Keep the roll of cookie dough wrapped tightly in plastic wrap in the freezer. Slice off and bake cookies as you need them.

1. Preheat the oven to 375°F.

2. Coat the cookie sheets with nonstick cooking spray or cover with parchment paper or a silicone baking mat.

3. Sift together the flour, baking soda, salt, cinnamon, and ginger. Set aside.

4. Cream the butter. Beat in the espresso powder, sucralose–brown sugar blend, dark brown sugar, agave syrup, and egg. With the mixer on the lowest speed, gradually add the flour mixture, scraping down the sides of the bowl as necessary and beating only until thoroughly mixed.

5. Press the dough into a roll about 12 inches long and 1½ inches in diameter. Wrap the dough tightly in plastic wrap and freeze until very firm.

6. Slice the dough ⅛ inch thin and place on the prepared cookie sheets. Bake until the edges start to brown, 10 minutes. Transfer to a rack to cool.

Nutritional Information Per Cookie: Calories 43, Protein 1 g, Carbohydrates 6 g, Fiber 0.5 g, Total Fat 2 g, Saturated Fat 1 g, Sodium 23 mg

MAKES 54 COOKIES

2 cups white whole wheat flour

½ teaspoon baking soda

½ teaspoon kosher salt

1 teaspoon ground cinnamon

½ teaspoon ground ginger

4 ounces unsalted butter

2 teaspoons espresso powder

2½ tablespoons sucralose–brown sugar blend

⅓ cup dark brown sugar

⅓ cup agave syrup

1 egg

Dark Chocolate–Glazed Oatmeal Cookies

These cookies were inspired by the Dark Chocolate Florentines in the November/December 2008 *Eating Well* magazine. You can almost call them health food when you consider all their nutritional strengths: soluble fiber from the oats, omega-3 fatty acids from the walnuts, reduced sugar and low glycemic impact sweetener, and antioxidants from the dark chocolate.

1. Preheat the oven to 375°F.

2. Line two baking sheets with parchment paper or silicone baking mats.

3. Melt the butter in a medium saucepan. Remove from the heat. Add the walnut oil, canola oil, oats, flour, sugar blend, agave syrup, espresso, vanilla, salt, and walnut meal. Mix well.

4. Drop level tablespoons of dough 2 inches apart on the prepared baking sheets. Press each cookie with a spatula to flatten.

5. Bake the cookies until edges are lightly browned, 12 to 15 minutes. Allow the cookies to cool completely on the baking sheet. Meanwhile, melt the chocolate in a double boiler.

6. Top each cookie with a ½ teaspoon of the melted chocolate. Allow to cool and serve.

Nutritional Information Per Cookie: Calories 94, Protein 1 g, Carbohydrates 9 g, Fiber 1 g, Total Fat 6.5 g, Saturated Fat 3 g, Sodium 6 mg

MAKES ABOUT 3 DOZEN TWO-INCH COOKIES

⅓ cup unsalted butter

2 tablespoons walnut oil

2 tablespoons canola oil

2 cups old-fashioned oats

⅓ cup whole wheat flour

¼ cup no-calorie sweetener and cane sugar blend

3 tablespoons agave syrup

¼ cup brewed espresso, cooled

1 teaspoon vanilla extract

½ teaspoon kosher salt

¾ cup walnuts, finely ground into a meal

6 ounces dark chocolate

Carrot Cake Cookies with Cream Cheese Drizzle

This recipe was inspired by the 24-karat cookies in Maida Heatter's *Book of Great Cookies* (Knopf, 1977). I substituted whole wheat pastry flour for the all-purpose flour and agave syrup for the honey to lower the glycemic impact. The addition of fresh ginger and the cream cheese drizzle makes the flavors a little more contemporary.

1. Preheat the oven to 350°F. Coat your cookie sheets with nonstick cooking spray or cover with parchment paper or a silicone baking mat.

2. Sift together the flour, baking powder, baking soda, cinnamon, and salt. Set aside.

3. Cream the butter. Beat in the egg and vanilla. Beat in the agave syrup, then the carrots and ginger. With the mixer on low speed, gradually add the flour mixture. When all of the flour mixture is added, beat in the oats, scraping down the sides of the bowl as necessary and beating only until thoroughly mixed. Stir in the currants and walnuts.

4. Using a 1-tablespoon-capacity scoop place the dough two inches apart on the prepared cookie sheets. Bake until golden brown and the tops spring back if lightly pressed with a fingertip, about 13 minutes. Use a metal spatula to transfer the cookies to racks to cool.

5. For the drizzle, beat together the cream cheese, vanilla, agave syrup, salt, evaporated milk, and ginger until smooth. Add more milk as needed to get the consistency right for drizzling. Place in a small squeeze bottle and drizzle over the cookies.

Nutritional Information Per Cookie: Calories 70, Protein 1 g, Carbohydrates 8 g, Fiber 0.5 g, Total Fat 4 g, Saturated Fat 2 g, Sodium 70 mg

MAKES 40 TWO-INCH COOKIES

CARROT CAKE COOKIES

1 cup whole wheat pastry flour

1 teaspoon baking powder

1 teaspoon baking soda

½ teaspoon ground cinnamon

¼ teaspoon kosher salt

4 ounces (1 stick) unsalted butter, soft

1 egg

½ teaspoon vanilla extract

½ cup agave syrup

½ cup raw grated carrots, firmly packed (about 3 carrots)

1 teaspoon grated ginger

½ cup old-fashioned oats

⅓ cup dried currants

¾ cup chopped walnuts

CREAM CHEESE DRIZZLE

4 ounces light cream cheese

½ teaspoon vanilla extract

1 tablespoon agave syrup

⅛ teaspoon kosher salt

2 tablespoons evaporated 2% milk, plus more as needed

⅛ teaspoon finely minced ginger

Pecan Cookies

This recipe is a variation of Maida Heatter's Plantation Pecan Cookies from her 1982 *Book of Great Desserts* (Knopf). I've added some cinnamon and changed the sweetener and flour to lower the glycemic impact of these cookies. Two of these cookies with a cup of spiced tea is a great 10-gram carbohydrate treat.

MAKES 22 COOKIES

4 ounces chopped pecans (about 1 cup)

4 ounces (1 stick) butter blend (trans-fat free)

½ teaspoon vanilla extract

¼ teaspoon kosher salt

¼ cup sucralose granulated sweetener

1½ teaspoons brewed coffee, cooled

1 cup white whole wheat flour, sifted

1 teaspoon ground cinnamon

2 teaspoons granulated sugar

22 pecan halves

Dusting of confectioners' sugar *(optional)*

1. Preheat the oven to 375°F.

2. Grind the chopped pecans in a blender into a coarse meal. Set aside.

3. Cream the butter blend. Beat in the vanilla, salt, and sucralose. Continue to beat for about 1 to 2 minutes until light and fluffy. Beat in the coffee.

4. With the mixer on low speed, gradually add the flour and ½ teaspoon of the cinnamon scraping down the sides of the bowl as necessary and beating until smooth.

5. Add the ground pecan meal and beat until incorporated.

6. Chill the dough until it is firm enough to handle, about 20 minutes.

7. Mix the remaining ½ teaspoon cinnamon and the granulated sugar. Shape the dough into 22 small balls and roll in the cinnamon sugar. Place the cookie balls on an ungreased cookie sheet and press a pecan half firmly into the top of each cookie, flattening it slightly.

8. Bake until golden brown, about 20 minutes. Use a metal spatula to transfer the cookies to a rack to cool thoroughly. Dust with confectioners' sugar just before serving, if desired.

Note Once the cookies have been rolled into balls they can be stored in an airtight container and frozen. Bake them a few at a time after defrosting.

Nutritional Information Per Cookie: Calories 101, Protein 1 g, Carbohydrates 5 g, Fiber 1 g, Total Fat 9 g, Saturated Fat 2 g, Sodium 50 mg

Chocolate Cereal Crumbles

So simple, so satisfying, these treats can be made with any high-protein, high-fiber cereal.

¼ cup semisweet chocolate chips

½ cup high-protein high-fiber cereal

2 tablespoons Spanish peanuts

1. Melt the chocolate in a glass dish in the microwave, about 1½ minutes. Stir and microwave an additional 20 to 30 seconds until fully melted.

2. Stir in the cereal and peanuts and drop by the tablespoonful onto parchment paper. Allow to harden at room temperature. Once the chocolate is hard, store the cereal crumbles in an airtight container for up to a week.

Nutritional Information Per Serving: Calories 114, Protein 4 g, Carbohydrates 14 g, Fiber 2.5 g, Total Fat 6 g, Saturated Fat 3 g, Sodium 31 mg

Chocolate-Dipped Pretzels

This is another quick way to make a sweet treat. Coarse sea salt sprinkled on the chocolate makes the flavor pop.

1. In a small, narrow cup, melt the dark chocolate in the microwave, about 1½ minutes. Stir the chocolate and microwave an additional 20 to 30 seconds until fully melted.

2. Dip the pretzel sticks in the melted chocolate, twirling the sticks along the side of the cup to remove excess chocolate.

3. Place the coated pretzels onto parchment paper and sprinkle with the salt. Allow the chocolate to harden at room temperature before serving.

Nutritional Information Per Serving: Calories 165, Protein 3 g, Carbohydrates 27 g, Fiber 3 g, Total Fat 6 g, Saturated Fat 2.5 g, Sodium 600 mg

MAKES 2 SERVINGS

¼ cup semisweet chocolate chips

Ten 3-inch-long multigrain pretzel sticks (with 2 to 3 g fiber per serving)

⅛ teaspoon coarse sea salt

Sweet Potato Panna Cotta with Toasted Pecans and Cranberry Coulis

This is a sophisticated alternative to pumpkin pie.

MAKES 6 SERVINGS

1. Mix the gelatin in water and allow to sit for 5 minutes until it starts gelling.

2. Melt the gelatin in a double boiler and add the ricotta-yogurt cream. Allow to steep for 15 minutes.

3. Coat 6 small molds with cooking spray and a dusting of confectioners' sugar. Fill the molds with the cream mixture and chill until set.

4. Pool 2 tablespoons cranberry coulis on 6 serving plates. Briefly soak the molds in hot water and invert over the coulis.

5. Garnish each serving with 1 tablespoon chopped pecans.

Nutritional Information Per Serving: Calories 130, Protein 3 g, Carbohydrates 18 g, Fiber 2.5 g, Total Fat 5 g, Saturated Fat 1 g, Sodium 53 mg

1½ teaspoons gelatin

1⅓ cups Ricotta-Yogurt Cream Dessert Base (page 202)

2 tablespoons water

¾ cup Cranberry Coulis (recipe below)

6 tablespoons chopped pecans, toasted

Cranberry Coulis

This coulis is sweet and tart—an excellent complement to a variety of desserts.

MAKES ¾ CUP

1. Bring all the ingredients to a simmer and cook until the cranberries have popped and the sauce has thickened slightly. Strain the sauce.

2. Allow the coulis to cool before serving with the panna cotta.

Nutritional Information Per 2 Tablespoon Serving of Coulis: Calories 40, Protein 0 g, Carbohydrates 9 g, Fiber 1.5 g, Total Fat 0 g, Saturated Fat 0 g, Sodium 3 mg

2 cups fresh cranberries

⅓ cup sugar-free vanilla-flavored syrup

½ teaspoon orange zest

2 tablespoons sucralose–brown sugar blend

¼ cup fresh orange juice

Ricotta-Yogurt Cream Dessert Base

This dessert base can be used to make panna cotta or ice cream. The sweet potatoes and agave syrup keep the glycemic impact low. It can be stored in the refrigerator for up to 7 days.

Purée all the ingredients in a blender or food processor until smooth.

Note For a frozen dessert (glacé), freeze the purée in an ice cream machine following manufacturer's instructions.

Nutritional Information Per ½ cup Serving: Calories 212, Protein 8 g, Carbohydrates 37 g, Fiber 1 g, Total Fat 4 g, Saturated Fat 2.5 g, Sodium 229 mg

MAKES SIX SERVINGS

1¼ cups part-skim ricotta

¾ cup plain nonfat Greek yogurt

⅔ cup agave syrup

1 cup mashed cooked sweet potato

2 teaspoons vanilla extract

1 teaspoon maple extract

1 teaspoon ground cinnamon

¼ teaspoon ground nutmeg

¼ teaspoon ground allspice

Sweet Vanilla Noodle Pudding

Besides making a nice, homey dessert, this noodle pudding is great part of a brunch buffet.

1¼ teaspoons kosher salt

7 ounces low-glycemic impact pasta, ziti or rotelle shaped

1 cup nonfat sour cream

4 ounces light cream cheese

One 15-ounce container part-skim ricotta

2 eggs

6 tablespoons sucralose granulated sweetener

2 tablespoons sucralose–brown sugar blend

2 teaspoons vanilla extract

2 teaspoons ground cinnamon

¼ teaspoon kosher salt

1 tablespoon dark brown sugar

¼ cup chopped walnuts

1 tablespoon all-purpose flour

1 tablespoon unsalted butter

1. Preheat the oven to 325° F. Coat an 8-inch square pan with non-stick cooking spray.

2. Bring a pot of water and 1 teaspoon of the salt to a boil. Add the pasta and cook according to package instructions. Do not overcook. Drain the pasta and reserve.

3. Mix the sour cream, cream cheese, ricotta, eggs, sucralose, sucralose–brown sugar blend, vanilla, 1 teaspoon of the cinnamon, and remaining salt until smooth and well blended.

4. Add the cooked pasta and mix well. Place the mixture in the prepared pan and bake for 1 hour.

5. Meanwhile, use your fingers to mix the dark brown sugar, walnuts, flour, butter, and the remaining 1 teaspoon cinnamon until the mixture resembles a coarse meal.

6. Top the pudding with the walnut mixture and bake for 15 minutes more. Serve warm.

Nutritional Information Per Serving: Calories 275, Protein 12 g, Carbohydrates 18 g, Fiber 2 g, Total Fat 12 g, Saturated Fat 6 g, Sodium 313 mg

Lemon, Ginger, Barley Pudding with Raspberries

This is a sophisticated variation of rice pudding and one of my favorite desserts. It also makes a great sweet treat at breakfast. You can make it using leftover barley, too.

1. For the barley pudding: Combine all the ingredients in a heavy saucepan. Bring to a simmer and cook, stirring frequently, 8 to 10 minutes.

2. Remove from the heat and fold in the frozen berries. Allow to cool.

3. Meanwhile, for the lemon-ginger cream: Combine the ingredients and simmer for 5 minutes. Allow to cool and remove the ginger slices.

4. Use a ½ cup scoop to portion the barley pudding into individual ramekins. Top each with 1 tablespoon lemon-ginger cream and serve.

Nutritional Information Per Serving: Calories 138, Protein 1 g, Carbohydrates 29 g, Fiber 2 g, Total Fat 3 g, Saturated Fat 1.5 g, Sodium 71 mg

MAKES 6 SERVINGS

BARLEY PUDDING

2 cups cooked pearled barley

1 cup unsweetened almond-cashew cream

1 teaspoon vanilla extract

¼ cup agave syrup

Pinch freshly grated nutmeg

¼ teaspoon ground cinnamon

1 teaspoon lemon zest

½ teaspoon minced ginger

¾ cup frozen, unsweetened raspberries

LEMON-GINGER CREAM

6 tablespoons unsweetened almond-cashew cream

1 tablespoon agave syrup

½ teaspoon lemon zest

1-inch length ginger, peeled and sliced

Cheese Blintzes with Clementines Poached in Red Wine

You can serve these blintzes for brunch as well as a dessert.

1. Preheat the oven to 350°F.

2. For the whole wheat crêpes: Mix all the ingredients well with a whisk until no lumps remain.

3. Heat a small, nonstick frying pan or a nonstick crêpe pan over medium-high heat. Using about 3 to 4 tablespoons batter for each crêpe, ladle the batter into the pan and swirl to coat the pan evenly. Cook until the edges of the crêpe are lightly browned, 2 to 3 minutes. Flip the crêpe over and cook until the second side is golden.

4. Stack the crêpes between parchment paper and chill until ready to fill.

5. For the filling: Combine all the ingredients and blend until smooth. Keep chilled until ready to fill the crêpes.

6. Fill each crêpe with 3 tablespoons of the cheese filling. Fold in the edges and roll up like a burrito to form a sealed package. Bake until the center of a filled crêpe reads 145°F on an instant-read thermometer, about 40 minutes. Dust finished blintzes with the cinnamon. Set aside and keep warm.

7. For the poaching liquid: Combine all ingredients except the clementines in a tall, narrow saucepan. Bring to a simmer.

8. Rub the peeled whole clementines with a dry towel to remove any pith on the outside of the fruit.

9. Add them to the poaching liquid and simmer for 10 minutes turning the fruit as needed so all of it is exposed to the poaching liquid. Remove from heat and allow to cool.

10. Remove the clementines and slice into 3 sections horizontally. Strain the poaching liquid and bring to a boil. Reduce by at least half until it is the consistency of a syrup. Drizzle the syrup over the blintzes and serve with 2 clementine slices.

Nutritional Information Per Serving: Calories 274, Protein 11 g, Carbohydrates 37 g, Fiber 3 g, Total Fat 5 g, Saturated Fat 2.5 g, Sodium 315 mg

WHOLE WHEAT CRÊPES
¾ cup plus 1 tablespoon whole wheat pastry flour

1 cup plus 1 tablespoon 1% milk

1 egg

1 teaspoon agave syrup

½ teaspoon vanilla extract

⅛ teaspoon kosher salt

CHEESE BLINTZ FILLING
½ cup nonfat cottage cheese

½ cup nonfat ricotta

½ cup light cream cheese

2 tablespoons sucralose–brown sugar blend

½ teaspoon vanilla extract

½ teaspoon orange zest

¼ teaspoon kosher salt

1 egg, lightly beaten

Ground cinnamon for dusting

RED WINE–TEA POACHING LIQUID
1 cup red wine, such as Gamay or Pinot Noir

2 cups brewed chai spice tea

1 cinnamon stick

2 cloves

1 star anise

3 black peppercorns

1 tablespoon sucralose–brown sugar blend sweetener

2 tablespoons sugar-free, vanilla-flavored syrup

2 tablespoons agave syrup

¼ teaspoon orange zest

4 clementines, peeled

Chocolate Beer Cake with Dark Chocolate Ganache

Chef Hubert Martini at The Culinary Institute of America gave me this recipe. I made a few modifications to reduce the saturated fat but keep the richness of this chocolate cake.

1. Preheat the oven to 350°F.

2. Cut a piece of parchment paper to cover the bottom of 10-inch springform pan. Coat the parchment with nonstick cooking spray, dust with flour, and place sprayed side up in the pan.

3. Mix the flour, baking soda, cinnamon, and salt and set aside. Melt the butter and butter blend. Whisk in the beer, cocoa powder, and vanilla. Allow to cool to room temperature.

4. Mix the sucralose–brown sugar blend and granulated sucralose with an electric mixer. Slowly add in the beer-chocolate mixture alternating with the flour mixture.

5. Add the eggs and yogurt. Spread the batter in the prepared pan. Bake until a knife inserted in center of cake comes out clean, about 35 minutes. Do not overbake.

6. While the cake is cooling, prepare the ganache: Bring the almond-cashew cream, beer, agave syrup, sucrolase, and cocoa powder to a simmer. Pour over the chocolate and stir until the chocolate is melted and the ganache is smooth.

7. When the cake is cool, slice the cake in half horizontally and spread one-third of the ganache on bottom half. Replace the top half of cake and frost with the remaining ganache.

Nutritional Information Per Serving: Calories 357, Protein 6.5 g, Carbohydrates 42 g, Fiber 4.5 g, Total Fat 19 g, Saturated Fat 10 g, Sodium 266 mg

MAKES 16 SERVINGS

3 cups whole wheat pastry flour

2 teaspoons baking soda

1 teaspoon ground cinnamon

½ teaspoon kosher salt

4 ounces (1 stick) unsalted butter

1 stick butter blend (trans-fat free)

1¼ cups dark beer

1 cup unsweetened cocoa powder

½ teaspoon vanilla extract

½ cup sucralose–brown sugar blend

½ cup granulated sucralose

3 eggs

6-ounce container of nonfat plain Greek yogurt

GANACHE

⅔ cup almond-cashew cream

¼ cup dark beer

1 tablespoon agave syrup

2 teaspoons granulated sucralose

2 tablespoons unsweetened cocoa powder

4 ounces sugar-free dark chocolate

6 ounces semisweet chocolate

Sweet Potato Waffle with Ice Cream

Serve with a scoop of your favorite no-sugar-added ice cream; butter pecan is especially good with these waffles. The waffles also freeze well and can be reheated in the toaster.

1. Combine the flour, baking powder, baking soda, salt, ginger, cinnamon, and sucralose–brown sugar blend. Set aside. Combine the sweet potato, buttermilk, butter, walnut or pecan oil, egg yolks, and vanilla. Stir the flour mixture into the sweet potato mixture.

2. Whisk the egg whites until stiff. Fold them into the batter.

3. Heat the waffle iron and grease with some of the canola oil before cooking each waffle. Ladle about ¾ cup of the batter onto the center of the hot waffle iron. Cook until the waffle is golden brown and crispy, about 3 minutes per side.

4. Cut each waffle into 4 sections and serve each section with a ½ cup ice cream and garnish with 1 teaspoon chopped pecans.

Nutritional Information Per Serving: Calories 197, Protein 6 g, Carbohydrates 24 g, Fiber 3 g, Total Fat 8 g, Saturated Fat 3 g, Sodium 155 mg

MAKES 16 SERVINGS

1 cup white whole wheat flour

1 teaspoon baking powder

¼ teaspoon baking soda

½ teaspoon kosher salt

1 teaspoon ground ginger

1 teaspoon ground cinnamon

¼ cup sucralose–brown sugar blend

1 cup mashed cooked sweet potato

1 cup low-fat buttermilk

1 tablespoon unsalted butter, melted

1 tablespoon walnut *or* pecan oil

2 large eggs, separated

½ teaspoon vanilla extract

1 tablespoon canola oil

2 quarts no-sugar added ice cream

⅓ cup pecans, toasted and chopped

Mini Popovers with Peaches and Blueberries

When peaches and blueberries are abundant and sweet during the summer, buy extra and freeze them in one-cup portions for the off-season. Peel and cut the peaches into cubes and place in a single layer on a baking sheet to freeze them. Layer the blueberries the same way after washing them and drying with paper towels. Once the fruit is frozen you can transfer it to small freezer bags.

1. Preheat the oven to 450°F.

2. Grease a standard, 12-cup muffin tin with cooking spray, or grease a nonstick, mini-popover pan for even easier removal.

3. Whisk together the flour, cinnamon, and salt.

4. Whisk together the eggs, milk, ½ teaspoon of the vanilla, and 1 tablespoon of the melted butter.

5. Pour the egg mixture over the flour mixture and fold just until blended. A few small lumps may remain.

6. Fill the muffin cups two-thirds full. Bake for 15 minutes in the center of the oven, then lower the heat to 350°F and bake until well browned and crusty, about 20 minutes more. Do not open the oven before the last 5 minutes of baking to avoid deflating the popovers.

7. Meanwhile, chop the peaches into ½-inch pieces and mix with the frozen blueberries.

8. Toss the fruit mixture with the brown sugar and the remaining ½ teaspoon vanilla. Allow to defrost until the last 5 minutes of cooking.

9. Sauté the fruit in the remaining melted butter until the syrup is reduced. Toss with the lemon juice and keep warm until popovers are done.

10. Remove popovers from the oven, unmold onto a rack, and puncture the tops with sharp knife to allow steam to release. Serve popover upside down, filling the hollow with fruit and syrup.

Nutritional Information Per Serving: Calories 114, Protein 3.5 g, Carbohydrates 18 g, Fiber 1.5 g, Total Fat 3 g, Saturated Fat 2 g, Sodium 75 mg

MAKES 12 SERVINGS

1 cup all-purpose flour

½ teaspoon ground cinnamon

½ teaspoon kosher salt

2 large eggs, at room temperature

1¼ cups 1% milk, at room temperature

1 teaspoon vanilla extract

2 tablespoons unsalted butter, melted

3 cups unsweetened frozen peach slices

2 cups unsweetened frozen blueberries

2 tablespoons brown sugar, packed

1 teaspoon fresh lemon juice

Glossary

A

agave syrup A plant-based liquid sweetener similar to honey, but with less glycemic impact than honey.

amaranth A tiny grain with an aroma and flavor described as corn-like and woodsy. Its high starch content makes it more suitable for soups, stews, and porridges than drier pilaf-style preparations. Toasting the grain first and adding it to already boiling liquid prevents it from becoming gummy. Amaranth is high in protein, iron, calcium, and vitamin E.

antioxidants Naturally occurring substances that retard the breakdown of tissues in the presence of oxygen. May be added to food during processing or may occur naturally. Help to prevent food from becoming rancid or discolored due to oxidation.

aromatics Ingredients, such as herbs, spices, vegetables, citrus fruits, wines, and vinegars, used to enhance the flavor and fragrance of food.

B

bake To cook food by surrounding it with dry heat in a closed environment, as in an oven.

barley A grain that is most commonly available as pearled barley (hull and bran removed). Also available unpolished (Scotch or pot barley) or as a flour.

baste To moisten food during cooking with pan drippings, sauce, or other liquid. Basting prevents food from drying out.

bisque A soup based on crustaceans or a vegetable purée. It is classically thickened with rice and usually finished with cream.

blanch To cook an item briefly in boiling water or hot fat before finishing or storing it. Blanching preserves the color, lessens strong flavors, and helps remove the peels of some fruits and vegetables.

boil A cooking method in which items are immersed in liquid at or above the boiling point (212°F / 100°C).

bouquet garni A small bundle of herbs tied with string. It is used to flavor broths, braises, and other preparations. Usually contains bay leaf, parsley, thyme, and possibly other aromatics wrapped in leek leaves.

braise A cooking method in which the main item, usually meat, is seared in fat, then simmered at a low temperature in a small amount of stock or another liquid (usually halfway up the meat item) in a covered vessel for a long time. The cooking liquid is then reduced and used as the base of a sauce.

bran The outer layer of a cereal grain and the part highest in fiber.

broil To cook by means of a radiant heat source placed above the food.

broth A flavorful, aromatic liquid made by simmering water or stock with meat, vegetables, and/or spices and herbs.

C

calorie A unit used to measure food energy. It is the amount of energy needed to raise the temperature of 1 kilogram of water by 1°C.

caramelization The process of browning sugar in the presence of heat. The caramelization of sugar occurs from 320° to 360°F / 160° to 182°C.

carbohydrate One of the basic nutrients used by the body as a source of energy. Types include simple (sugars) and complex (starches and fibers).

carryover cooking Heat retained in cooked foods that allows them to continue cooking even after removal from the cooking medium. Especially important to roasted foods.

cheesecloth A light, fine-mesh gauze used for straining liquids and making sachets.

chile The fruit of certain types of capsicum peppers (not related to black pepper), used fresh or dried as a seasoning. Chiles come in many types (e.g., jalapeño, serrano, poblano) and varying degrees of spiciness.

cholesterol A substance found exclusively in animal products such as meat, eggs, and cheese (dietary cholesterol) or in the blood (serum cholesterol).

chowder A thick soup that may be made from a variety of ingredients but usually contains potatoes.

clarification The process of removing solid impurities from a liquid (such as butter or broth). Also, a mixture of ground meat, egg whites, mirepoix, tomato purée, herbs, and spices used to clarify broth for consommé.

complete protein A food source that provides all of the essential amino acids in the correct ratio so that they can be used in the body for protein synthesis. May require more than one ingredient (such as beans and rice together).

complex carbohydrate A large molecule made up of long chains of sugar molecules. In food, these molecules are found in starches and fiber.

cornstarch A fine, white powder milled from dried corn; used primarily as a thickener for sauce and occasionally as an ingredient in batters.

cross-contamination The transfer of disease-causing elements from one source to another through physical contact.

D

danger zone The temperature range from 41° to 135°F / 5° to 57°C; the most favorable condition for rapid growth of many pathogens.

deglaze The use of a liquid, such as wine, water, or broth, to dissolve food particles and/ or caramelized drippings left in a pan after roasting or sautéing. The resulting mix then becomes the base for the accompanying sauce.

dredge To coat food with a dry ingredient such as flour or bread crumbs prior to frying or sautéing.

E

emulsion A mixture of two or more liquids, one of which is a fat or oil and the other of which is water based, so that tiny globules of one are suspended in the other. This may involve the use of stabilizers, such as egg or mustard. Emulsions may be temporary, permanent, or semipermanent.

evaporated milk Unsweetened canned milk from which 60 percent of the water has been removed before canning. It is often used in custards and to create a creamy texture in food.

F

fiber The structural component of plants that is necessary to the human diet and is indigestible. Also referred to as roughage. Fiber is divided into two categories: soluble and insoluble. Soluble fiber dissolves in water and regulates the body's use of sugar by slowing their digestion and release into the bloodstream. Insoluble fiber absorbs water, providing bulk in the diet and clears out the intestinal tract.

fond The French term for stock. Also describes the pan drippings remaining after sautéing or roasting food. It is often deglazed and used as a base for sauces.

food-borne illness An illness in humans caused by the consumption of an adulterated food product. For an official determination that an outbreak of food-borne illness has occurred, two or more people must have become ill after eating the same food, and the outbreak must be confirmed by health officials.

fructose A simple sugar found in fruits. Fructose is the sweetest simple sugar.

G

germ The portion of the seed of flowering plants, such as wheat, that sprouts to form a new plant; the embryo of the new plant.

glucose A simple sugar found in honey, some fruits, and many vegetables. It has about half the sweetness of table sugar and is the preferred source of energy for the human body.

grill A cooking technique in which foods are cooked by a radiant heat source placed below the food. Also, the piece of equipment on which grilling is done. Grills may be fueled by gas, electricity, charcoal, or wood.

H

hydrogenation The process in which hydrogen atoms are added to an unsaturated fat molecule, making it partially or completely saturated and solid at room temperature.

I

infusion Steeping an aromatic or other item in liquid to extract its flavor. Also, the liquid resulting from this process.

J

julienne Vegetables, potatoes, or other items cut into thin strips; ⅛ in by ⅛ in by 1 to 2 in / 3 mm by 3 mm by 3 to 5 cm is standard. Fine julienne is ¹⁄₁₆ in by ¹⁄₁₆ in by 1 to 2 in / 1.5 mm by 1.5 mm by 3 to 5 cm.

L

legume The seeds of certain pod plants, including beans and peas, which are eaten for their earthy flavors and high nutritional value. Also, the French word for vegetable.

M

mandoline A slicing device of stainless steel with carbon steel blades. The blades may be adjusted to cut items into various shapes and thicknesses.

marinade A mixture used before cooking to flavor and moisten foods; may be liquid or dry.

Liquid marinades are usually based on an acidic ingredient, such as wine or vinegar; dry marinades are usually salt based.

milling The process by which grain is separated into germ/husk, bran, and endosperm and ground into flour or meal.

mirepoix A combination of chopped aromatic vegetables—usually two parts onion, one part carrot, and one part celery—used to flavor broths, soups, braises, and stews.

monounsaturated fat A fat with one available bonding site not filled with a hydrogen atom. Helpful in lowering the LDL cholesterol level (the bad cholesterol). Food sources include avocados, olives, and nuts.

N

nutrient A basic component of food used by the body for growth, repair, restoration, and energy. Includes carbohydrates, fats, proteins, water, vitamins, and minerals.

nutrition The process by which an organism takes in and uses food.

O

oat A readily available and inexpensive grain that is high in fiber. Oats can be left whole (groats) or processed into oatmeal or oat bran. Oatmeal can be steel cut, rolled, quick cooking, instant, or made into flakes.

omega-3 fat A type of polyunsaturated fatty acids that may reduce the risk of heart disease and tumor growth, stimulate the immune system, and lower blood pressure. They occur in fatty fish and certain nuts, seeds, and oils.

P

pan steaming A method of cooking foods in a very small amount of liquid in a covered pan over direct heat.

parch Heating a grain in hot fat or oil in order to begin gelatinizing the starches.

parcook To partially cook an item before storing or finishing.

pilaf A technique for cooking grains in which the grain is sautéed briefly in butter then simmered in stock or water with various seasonings until the liquid is absorbed. Also called *pilau, pilaw, pullao, pilav.*

polyunsaturated fat A fat molecule with more than one available bonding site not filled with a hydrogen atom. Food sources include corn, cottonseed, safflower, soy, and sunflower oils.

purée To process food by mashing, straining, or chopping it very finely in order to make it a smooth paste. Also, a product produced using this technique.

Q

quinoa A grain with a mildly nutty flavor and intriguing texture. The germ, which completely surrounds the grain, falls away during cooking and remains slightly crunchy, while the grain itself becomes meltingly soft. This duality of texture makes quinoa like two grains in one. Quinoa is one of the quickest-cooking whole grains and is very high in protein, vitamin E, iron, zinc, potassium, calcium, and B vitamins.

R

reduce To decrease the volume of a liquid by simmering or boiling; used to provide a thicker consistency and/or concentrated flavors.

risotto Rice that is sautéed briefly in fat with onions and possibly other aromatics, then combined with broth—which is added in several additions—and stirred constantly, producing a creamy texture with grains that are still al dente.

roast A dry-heat cooking method where the item is cooked in an oven or on a spit over a fire.

roux Equal parts flour and a fat (usually butter) used to thicken liquids. Roux is cooked to varying degrees (white, blond, or brown), depending on its intended use. The darker the roux, the less thickening power it has, but the fuller the taste.

S

sachet d'épices Literally, "bag of spices." Aromatic ingredients encased in cheesecloth and used to flavor stocks and other liquids. A standard sachet contains parsley stems, cracked peppercorns, dried thyme, and a bay leaf.

saturated fat A fat molecule whose available bonding sites are entirely filled with hydrogen atoms. These tend to be solid at room temperature and are primarily of animal origin, though coconut oil, palm oil, and cocoa butter are vegetable sources of saturated fat. Animal sources include butter, meat, cheese, and eggs.

sauté To cook quickly in a small amount of fat in a pan on the range top.

sear To brown the surface of food in fat over high heat before finishing by another method (e.g., braising or roasting) in order to add flavor.

simmer To maintain the temperature of a liquid just below boiling. Also, to cook in simmering liquid. The temperature range for simmering is 185° to 200°F / 85° to 93°C.

simple carbohydrate Any of a number of small carbohydrate molecules (mono- and disaccharides), including glucose, fructose, galactose, lactose, maltose, and sucrose.

slurry A starch, such as cornstarch or arrowroot, that is dissolved in cold liquid to prevent it from forming lumps when added to hot liquid as a thickener.

sodium An alkaline metal element necessary in small quantities for human nutrition; one of the components of most salts used in cooking.

spelt An ancient form of wheat that is more easily digestible and has a higher nutrition profile than standard wheat.

steam A cooking method in which items are cooked in a vapor bath created by boiling water or other liquids.

steep To allow an ingredient to sit in warm or hot liquid to extract flavor or impurities, or to soften the item.

stew A cooking method nearly identical to braising but generally involving smaller pieces of meat and hence a shorter cooking time. Stewed items also may be blanched, rather than seared, to give the finished product a pale color. Also, a dish prepared by using the stewing method.

stir-fry A cooking method similar to sautéing in which items are cooked over very high heat, using little fat. Usually this is done in a wok, and the food is kept moving constantly.

stock A flavorful liquid prepared by simmering meat bones, poultry bones, seafood bones, and/or vegetables in water with aromatics until their flavor is extracted. Used as a base for soups, sauces, and other preparations.

sweat To cook an item, usually vegetables, in a covered pan in a small amount of fat until it softens and releases moisture but does not brown.

T

trans fat A fat that is formed when liquid oils are processed into solids like shortening or margarine. Trans fats cause low-density lipoprotein levels to increase and high-density lipoprotein levels to decrease.

U

unsaturated fat A fat molecule with at least one available bonding site not filled with a hydrogen atom. These may be monounsaturated or polyunsaturated. They tend to be liquid at room temperature and are primarily of vegetable origin.

V

vegan An individual who has adopted a specific diet (or lifestyle) that eliminates animal products. Vegans eat no foods derived in any way from animals.

vegetarian An individual who has adopted a specific diet (or lifestyle) that reduces or eliminates animal products. Lacto-ovo vegetarians include dairy products and eggs in their diet. Ovo-vegetarians include eggs in their diet.

W

wheat berries Unrefined or minimally processed whole wheat kernels.

whole grain An unmilled or unprocessed grain.

Cooking Ratios and Times for Selected Pasta and Grains

Type	Ratio of Grain to Liquid (Cups)	Approximate Yield (Cups)	Cooking Time
Amaranth	1:2½ to 3	4	20 to 25 minutes
Barley, pearled	1:2	4	35 to 45 minutes
Buckwheat groats (kasha)	1:1½ to 2	2	12 to 20 minutes
Whole wheat couscous	1:1¼ to 1½	1½ to 2	5 to 10 minutes
Farro	1:2	3	30 to 35 minutes
Hominy, whole†	1:2½	3	2½ to 3 hours
Hominy grits	1:4	3	25 minutes
Millet	1:2	3	30 to 35 minutes
Oat groats	1:2	2	45 minutes to 1 hour
Polenta, firm	1:4	5	35 to 45 minutes
Polenta, soft	1:5	6	35 to 45 minutes
Quinoa	1:2	3	15 to 20 minutes
Rice, Carolina	1:1¾	3	25 to 30 minutes
Rice, long-grain, brown	1:3	4	40 minutes
Rice, short-grain, brown	1:2½	4	30 to 35 minutes
Rice, wild	1:4	5	40 to 45 minutes
Rye berries	1:3½	4	1 hour
Spelt	1:2	3	40 minutes
Wheat berries	1:3	2	1 hour
Wheat, bulgur, soaked‡	1:4	2	2 hours
Wheat, cracked§	1:2	3	20 minutes

†Grain should be soaked briefly in tepid water, then drained before it is steamed.
‡Grain should be soaked overnight in cold water, then drained before it is cooked.
§Grain may be cooked by covering it with boiling water and soaking for 2 hours, or by the pilaf cooking method.
The grains in color are whole grains.

Readings and Resources List

Books

Coppedge, Richard. *Gluten-Free Baking with The Culinary Institute of America.* Avon, MA: Adams Media, 2008.

The Culinary Institute of America. *Healthy Cooking At Home with The Culinary Institute of America.* Hoboken, NJ: John Wiley & Sons, 2011.

Dornenburg, Andrew, and Karen Page. *Culinary Artistry.* Hoboken, NJ: John Wiley & Sons, 1996.

Kolpan, Steven, Brian Smith, and Michael Weiss. *Wine Wise: Your Complete Guide to Understanding, Selecting and Enjoying Wine.* Hoboken, NJ: John Wiley & Sons, 2008.

Matthews, Brad, and Paul Wigsten. *Produce Identification, Fabrication, Utilization.* Clifton Park, NY: Delmar Cengage Learning, 2011.

Warshaw, Hope. *Complete Guide to Carb Counting: How to Take the Mystery out of Carb Counting and Improve your Blood Glucose Control.* Alexandria, VA: American Diabetics Association, 2011.

Websites

Academy of Nutrition and Dietetics (formerly the American Dietetic Association), Chicago, Illinois (www.eatright.org)

American Diabetes Association, Alexandria, Virginia (www.diabetes.org)

Agave International, Inc., Los Angeles, California (www.sweetcactusfarms.com)

Bob's Red Mill Natural Foods, Inc., Milwaukie, Oregon (www.bobsredmill.com)

Brykill Farms, Gardiner, New York (www.brykillfarm.com)

Hodgson Mill, Inc., Effingham, Illinois (www.hodgsonmill.com)

The King Arthur Flour Company, Inc., Norwich, Vermont (www.kingarthurflour.com)

Penzeys Spices, Wauwatosa, Wisconsin (www.penzeys.com)

Rancho Gordo New World Specialty Food, Napa, California (www.ranchogordo.com)

Whitecliff Winery, Gardiner, New York (www.whitecliffwine.com)

Zursun Idaho Heirloom Beans, Twin Falls, Idaho (www.zursunbeans.com)

Index

Page numbers in *italics* indicate illustrations

Orange(s), cont.
  Sesame, and Ginger Dressing,
    Multigrain Pasta with
    Broccolini, Red Bell Peppers,
    Crab Meat and, 92, *93*

P

Panna Cotta, Sweet Potato, with
    Toasted Pecans and Cranberry
    Coulis, 200, *201*
Pan searing technique, 72
Pan steaming technique, 132
Parmesan
  Grilled Tofu with Eggplant and, 80-
    81, *81*
  -Mushroom Salad, 99, 155
Parsley
  Chicken, and Quinoa Salad, *108*,
    109
  Cucumber, and Onion Salad with
    Feta, *104*, 144
  Frittata, and Toasted Walnut, 33
  and Lentil Salad with Mustard-
    Sherry Vinaigrette, *122*, 175
  -Mint Pesto, 34, *35*, *104*
  Tomato, and Feta Salad, 171
Pasta
  Fettuccine, Whole Wheat, with
    Tomato, Chicken, and Feta
    Cheese, 110, *111*
  Multigrain, with Broccolini, Red
    Bell Peppers, Crab Meat, and
    Orange, Sesame, and Ginger
    Dressing, 92, *93*
  Noodle Pudding, Sweet Vanilla, 203
  Spaghetti, Daikon, with Chicken and
    Tahini Soy Dressing, *112*, 113
  types of, 11
Peaches, Mini Popovers with
    Blueberries and, *210*, 211
Peas
  dry, soaking/cooking, 137
  sugar snap, 130
  Sugar Snap, with Champagne
    Vinaigrette, *100*, 160
  Tofu with Red Curry Paste, Green
    Onions, Cilantro and, *82*, 83
Pecan(s)
  Cookies, *194*, 195
  Quinoa and Nut–Stuffed Portobello
    Mushroom, 31, *107*

Strawberries with Dark Chocolate
    Glaze and, 188
Toasted, Sweet Potato Panna Cotta
    with Cranberry Coulis and,
    200, *201*
Peperonata, *122*, 149
Pepper(s). *See* Bell Pepper(s)
Pesto, Mint-Parsley, 34, *35*, *104*
Pilaf
  Barley and Couscous, *103*, 178
  basic technique, 138
  Mixed-Grain, *104*, 179
Poaching, shallow, 74, *94*
Poaching Liquid, Red Wine-Tea, 207
Popovers, Mini, with Peaches and
    Blueberries, *210*, 211
Pork. *See also* Meat
  Chorizo and Chickpea Soup, 54
  Sweet-'n'-Sour Pork-'n'-Beans, 121
  Tenderloin, Caraway-Herb Roasted,
    122, 123
Portobello Mushroom(s)
  in Mushroom Soup, Wild, 61
  Quinoa and Nut–Stuffed, 31, *107*
  in Turkey Meatloaf, 120
Portion control tools, 17
Pots and pans, 17
Poultry
  braising/stewing, 73
  grilling/broiling, 72
  roasting, 75
  sautéing, 72
  shallow poaching, 74
Pretzels, Chocolate-Dipped, *198*, 199
Protein, and meal planning, 70
Pudding(s)
  Barley, Lemon-Ginger, with
    Raspberries, 204, *205*
  Noodle, Sweet Vanilla, 203
Purée soups, 41-42

Q

Quinoa, 10. *See also* Grains
  and Black Bean–Stuffed Zucchini,
    78, 79
  Chicken, and Parsley Salad, *108*,
    109
  and Nut–Stuffed Portobello
    Mushroom, 31, *107*

R

Radishes, 130
  Daikon, –Sesame Salad, 157
  Daikon Spaghetti with Chicken and
    Tahini Soy Dressing, *112*, 113
  Roasted, *126*, 156
Raspberry(ies)
  Dressing, Arugula and Spinach
    Salad with, 140, *141*
  Steamed Kale with, 152, *153*
Red Bell Pepper(s). *See* Bell Pepper(s),
    Red
Red Curry Paste, Tofu with Peas,
    Green Onions, Cilantro and,
    82, 83
Red Wine
  Marinade, 80
  -Tea Poaching Liquid, 207
Rice, 11, 218. *See also* Grains
  in Mixed-Grain Pilaf, *104*, 179
Rice Paper, Shrimp and Asian
    Vegetables Wrapped in, 26
Ricotta
  in Cheese Blintzes with
    Clementines Poached in Red
    Wine, *206*, 207
  in Noodle Pudding, Sweet Vanilla,
    203
  -Yogurt Cream Dessert Base, 202
Risotto, basic technique for, 139
Roasting technique, 75, 134
Roll-Ups, Onion, Walnut, and Blue
    Cheese, 28, 29
Rub, Dry, 124

S

Salad(s)
  Artichoke, Hearts of, *168*, *169*, 169
  Arugula and Spinach, with
    Raspberry Dressing, 140, *141*
  Black-eyed Pea, *100*, 176
  Broccoli and Brussels Sprout Slaw,
    172
  Cabbage, Celery, and Carrot, with
    Sesame Dressing, 147
  Cabbage, Warm, 148
  Chayote, with Oranges, *67*, 164
  Chicken, Quinoa, and Parsley, *108*,
    109
  Cucumber, with Cider-Dijon
    Vinaigrette, 143